Rohim Ullah

Captured Dreams - An artist's soulful gaze on Rohingya

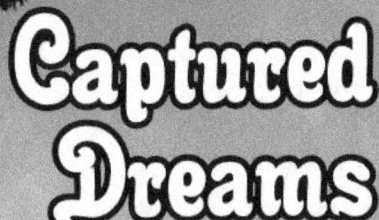

Captured Dreams

An artist's soulful gaze on Rohingya

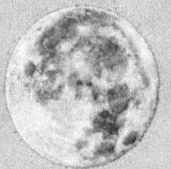

Rohim Ullah

Capturing Dreams from a bleak existence through the reflective Lens of Subjectivity

Captured Dreams
An artist's soulful gaze on
Rohingya

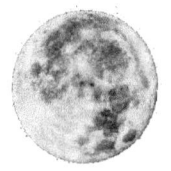

Rohim Ullah

This remarkable book of photography by Rohim Ullah is a poignant historical account, vividly capturing the adversity and superhuman strength of the Rohingya community within Cox's Bazaar, the world's largest refugee camp in Bangladesh.

ISBN: 9798867154806

Editor: Amy Dio Ramdass

Cover and book design: Amy Dio Ramdass

Pegasus Publishing
Ontario, Canada

"Refugees didn't just escape a place. They had to escape a thousand memories until they'd put enough time and distance between them and their misery to wake to a better day."
— Nadia Hashimi

Contents

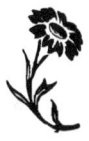

Visual Poetry

Dedication

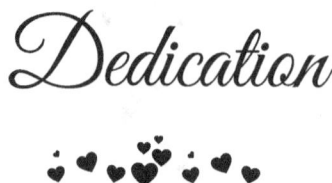

This book is dedicated to my family, friends, and loved ones who were lost during the Myanmar genocide.

It is also a tribute to my Rohingya people, who have endured decades of atrocities and genocide in Myanmar's Arakan state.

Your boundless courage and determination continue to inspire me.

Together, let us create a ripple effect of empathy and stand united in unwavering solidarity with the Rohingya community.

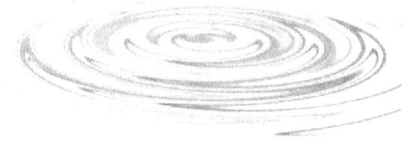

Biography

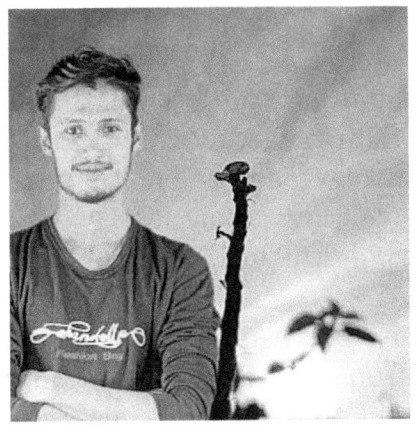

"Express what you are experiencing, don't hide it with your smile." ~*Rohim Ullah*

I am Rohim Ullah, a photojournalist, videographer, and frontline worker of the Rohingya community in the world's largest refugee camp at Cox's Bazar, Bangladesh.

Forced from my home in Myanmar (formerly Burma), where I owned a house, my family and I sought safety and survival in Bangladesh. I arrived here in 2017, fleeing Myanmar due to the brutal Burmese military operation that inflicted suffering and genocide upon the Rohingya people.

Currently, I have a job in an NGO where I have been working as a volunteer for the past five years. In addition, I engage in photography and videography, capturing the story of the Rohingya refugees in the camps at Cox's Bazar. Through my work, I aim to document the experiences of those in the refugee camps for a global audience.

I believe that one day, families will share their refugee stories with future generations. Not every camp has a dedicated photographer or photojournalist, limiting their ability to raise awareness and find solutions through this powerful medium.

My mission is to reveal the challenges we face in our daily lives, from the rudimentary and overcrowded shelters made of bamboo and plastic sheets to the dangers posed by the hilly landscape. I hope to highlight these issues with the aim of inspiring those with the capacity to help find solutions.

The region's lack of clean drinking water, rapid disease transmission, and inadequate sanitation are pressing issues. The annual rainy seasons exacerbate these problems, resulting in open sewage and flooding. In most seasons dengue fever and conjunctivitis diseases rage through the camps.

Many people have limited knowledge about refugees' life in camps. I hope that my skills and experiences can contribute to a better understanding of our situation and improve the lives of my fellow camp members.

Foreword

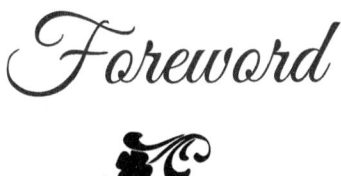

"**Legends are born in a valley of struggle.**"~Harshu Rao

I met Rohim Ullah, online, just days after learning of the Rohingya's genocide in Myanmar.

I was shocked to the roots of my core that such senseless (large-scale) brutality still persists in our modern era. Oh, the boundless ignorance of it all, the very shackle that the Buddha warned us of – our own ignorance.

Anyway, Rohim offered his photographs to complement any work of mine. Since I had no immediate need for photography, I promised to keep him in mind if the opportunity ever arose.

Rohim's photography left an indelible impression on me. Through the frames of his soulful captures, I saw in his gaze of subjectivity, all of the below and more.

The Road to Redemption
A Journey of Rebirth
A Quest for Revolution.
The Transformation of Earth!

Also, through his photos, I caught a glimpse of Rohim's 'considerate' personality, an adorable spirit, brimming with humor, empathy, and compassion.

After pondering the depths of possibility, an audacious thought took root in my mind. Could I, with my skills in magazine and book formatting, along with my experience in editing, transform this photographer into a storyteller? Could I encourage him to write poems so he may be a voice for the silenced Rohingya?

Rohim hesitated, doubting his own capacity. In fact, he was like, "I don't have any ideas for poetry." But I remained steadfast, for the notion of turning a non-author into an author felt like the purest form of magic.

I pitched the idea – to publish Rohim's photographs, enriched with empowering quotes, in a book. It appealed to him, as well as inspired him to craft a few poems, which you will discover within these pages.

And this is how a writer was born, the start of a new heroic journey, which goes to show that passion, inspiration and dedication can also give rise to LEGENDS.

Amy Dio Ramdass
Author/Editor/Publisher
Toronto, Ontario
Canada

Rohim Ullah

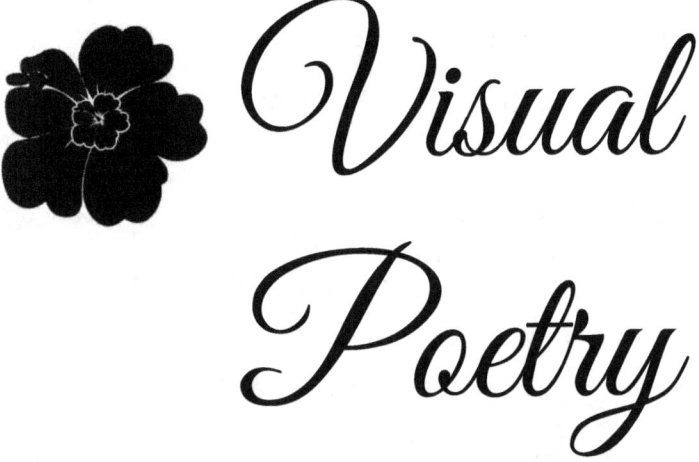

Visual Poetry

🌺 Soul Glimpses

"Keep showing your talent to the world. Let it not be for your own darkness but a beacon of light for your community." ~Rohim Mullah

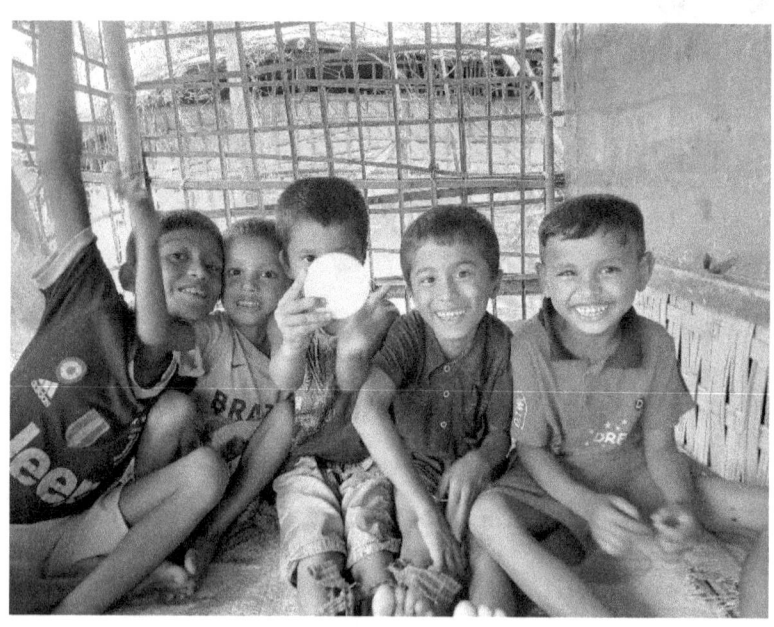

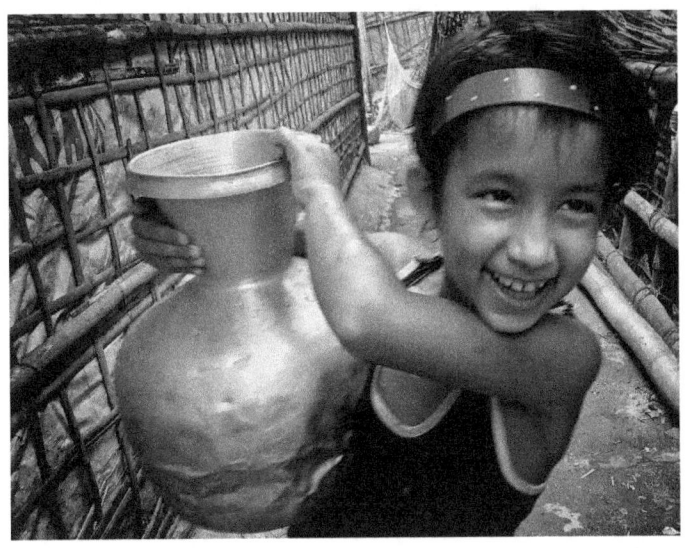

"**Smile, it's free therapy.**" ~ Douglas Horton

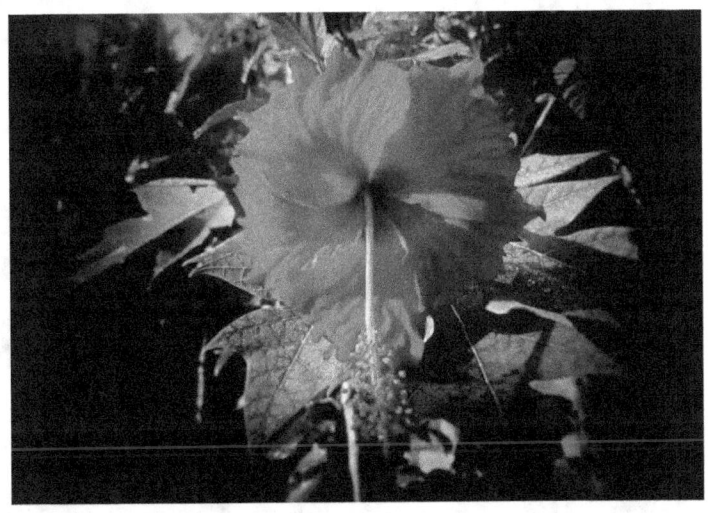

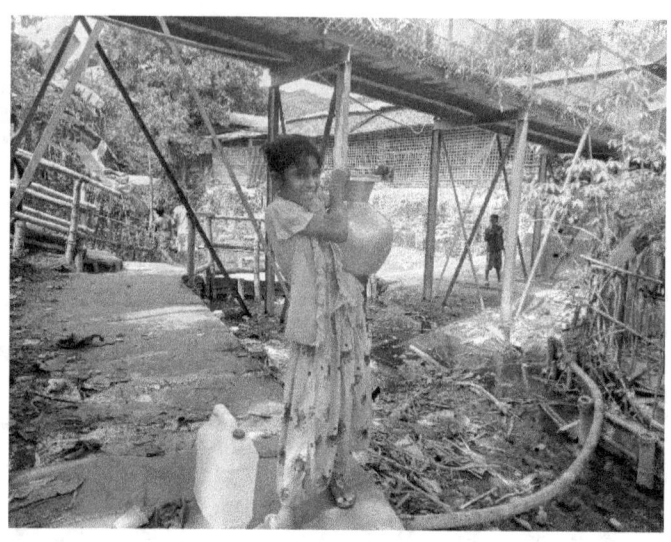

"Beauty is power; a smile is its sword." ~ John Ray

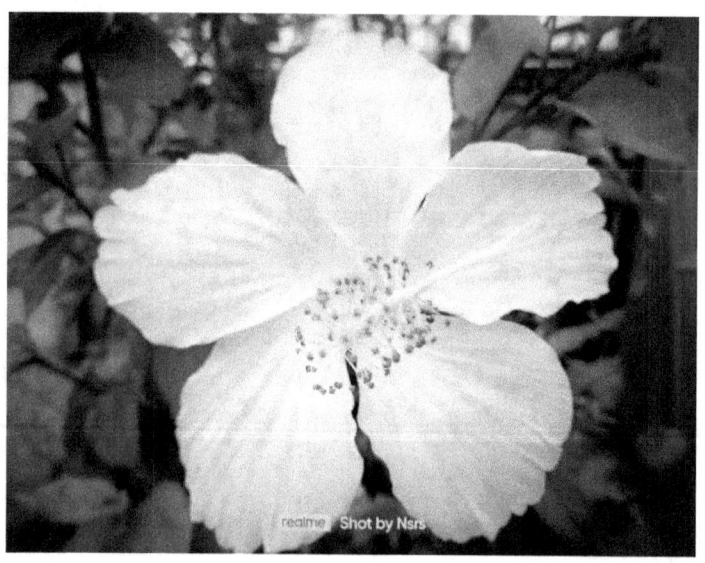

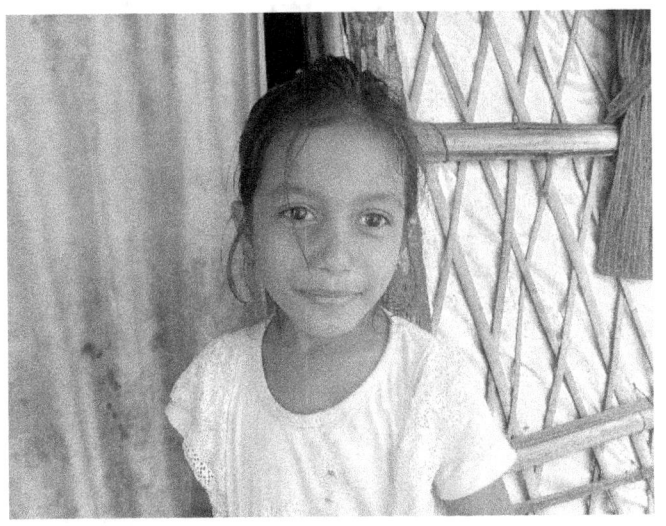

𝒜 smile is like a ray of sunshine
that brightens the stormiest of days,
casting warmth and radiance
on everything it touches.

"Peace begins with a smile."
– Mother Teresa

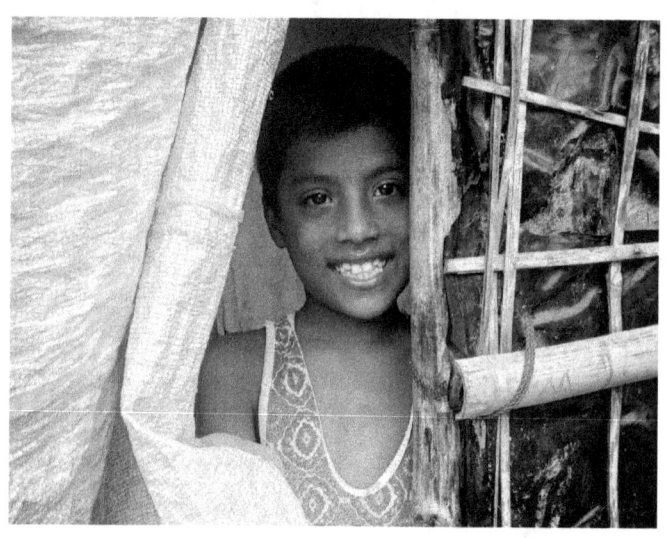

"I love those who can smile in trouble." - Leonardo da Vinci

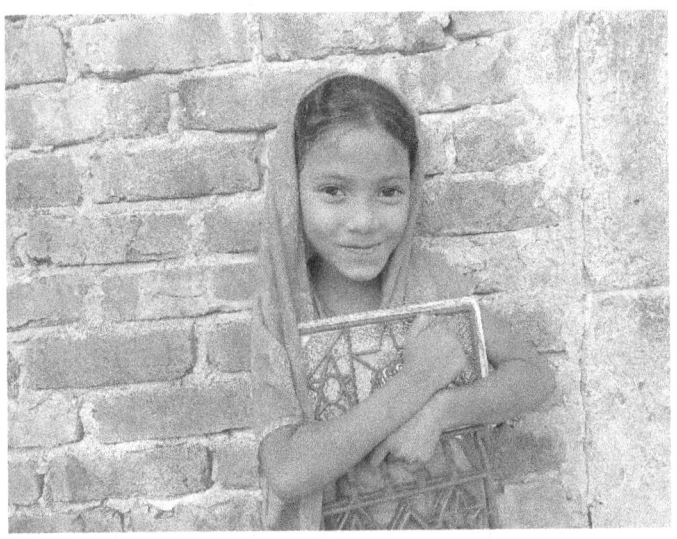

Like sunlit blossoms, they flower.
The smiles of Rohingya children
brightens the hour.

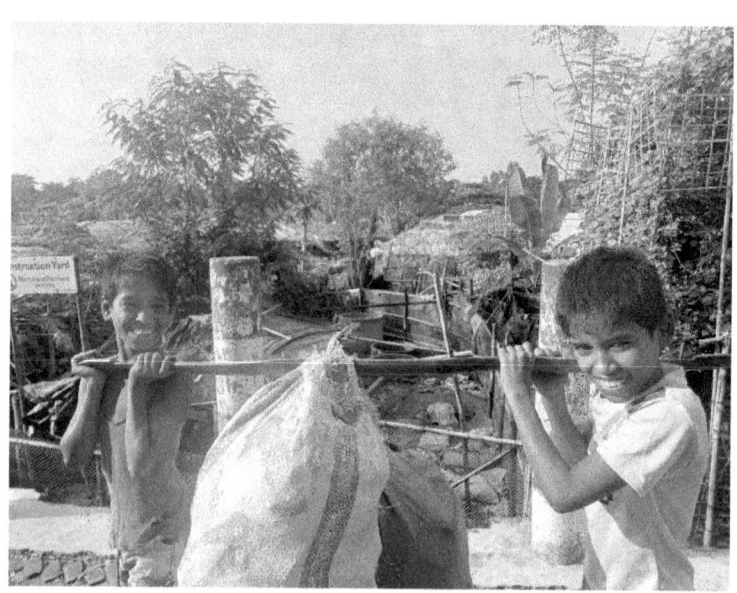

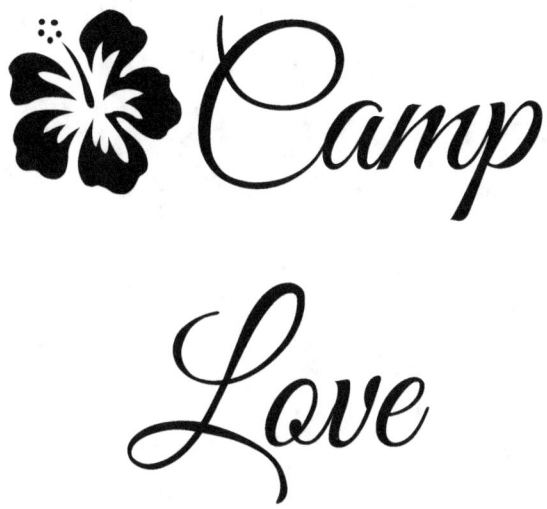

"To motivate your team, don't
display your superpowers.
Instead, show them, theirs."
~Rohim Mullah

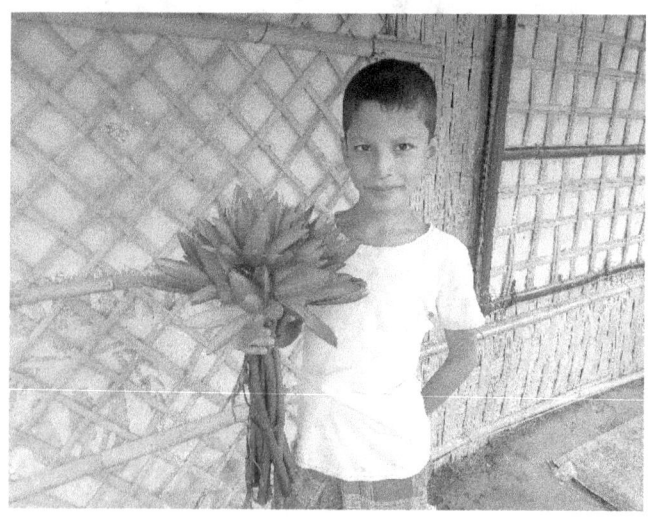

In the midst of adversity, he blooms,
a Rohingya boy with a lotus flower.

Hero's Welcome

"In this photo, I stand beside my beloved spiritual mentor, Mr. Md Osman Sorwar, UNHCR's senior field assistant in Bangladesh whom we absolutely adore.

He has already transferred from our camp to another camp but came to visit us today. I am smiling, but my heart is breaking because I am reminded of what he has done for me and my community." ~Rohim Ullah

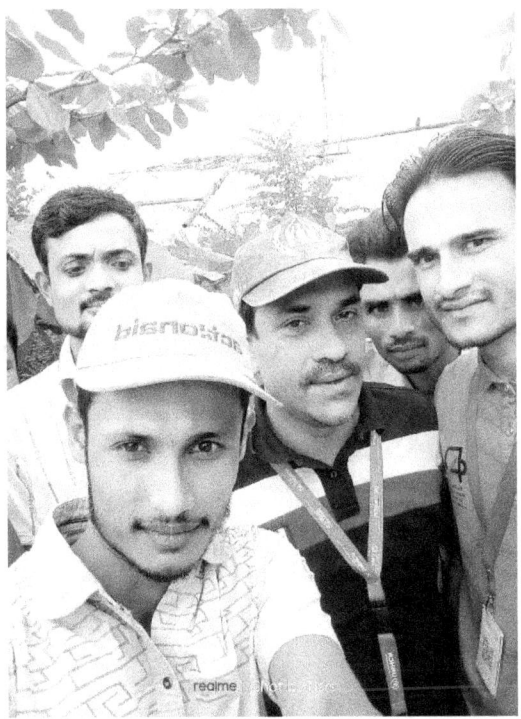

The author with more heroes

"It was a great moment with UNHCR's Mr Md Osman Sorwar and Mr Elias Sir at Rohingya Refugee Camp-26. Sometimes we meet with some kind-hearted and refugee-friendly people like Osman sir.

In the picture, you can see UNHCR's Mr Elias Sir with us who is very kind and refugee friendly person like Osman Sir." ~Rohim Ullah

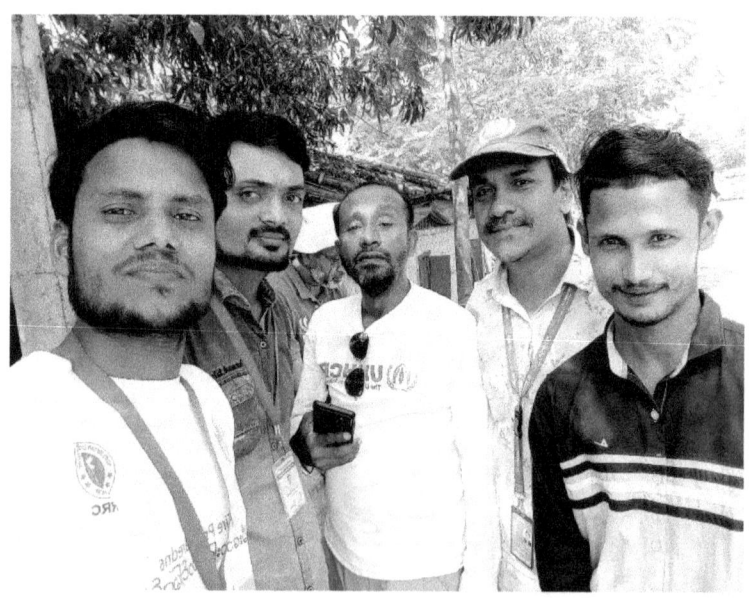

Little Heroes

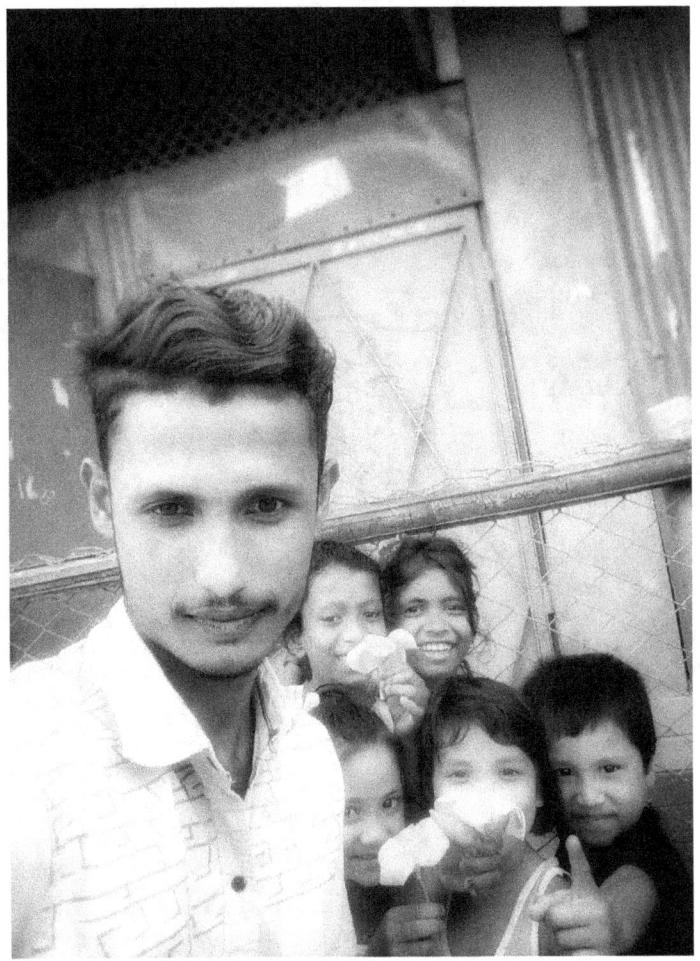

The author with future heroes

Friendship

Sweet smiles, like dawning Sunrise,
to dispel the shadows

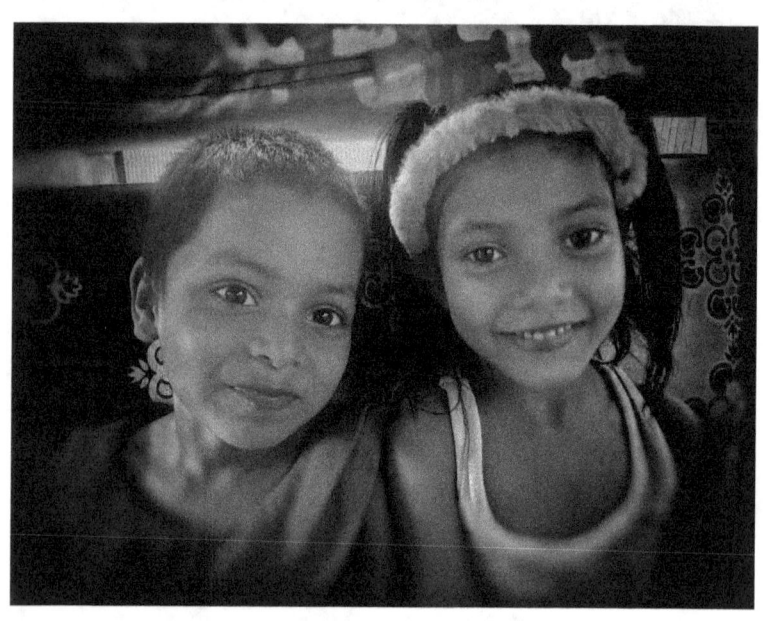

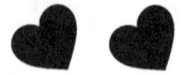

Flowers and Children are...

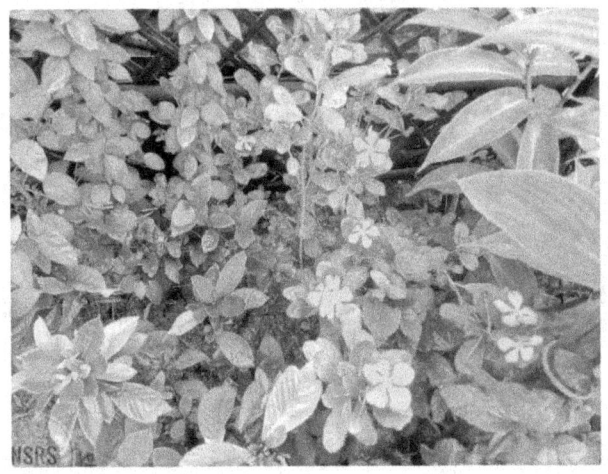

...Nature's love notes to the world

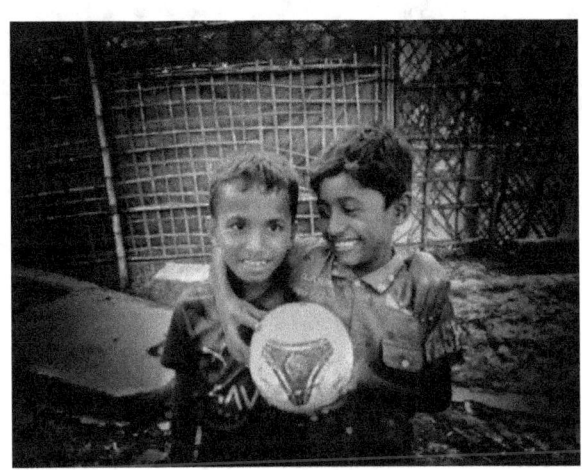

Selfie Time

The author and his amazing friends.

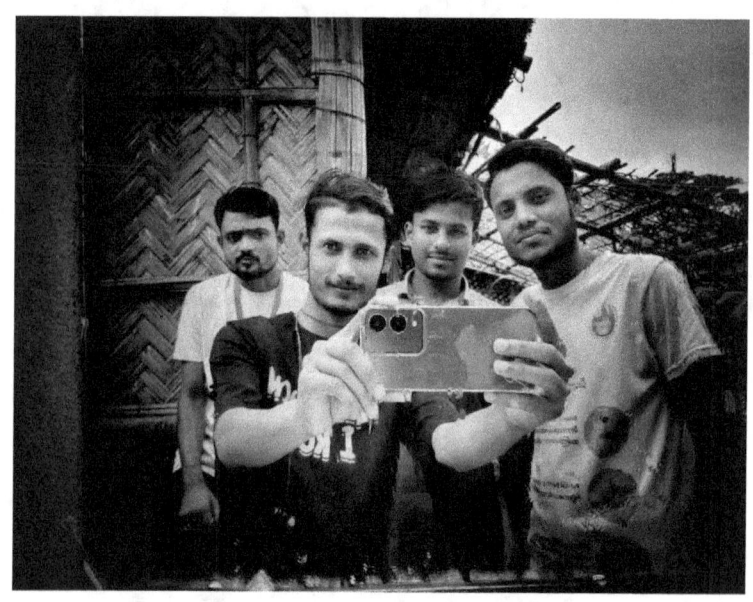

"Things are never quite as scary when you've got a best friend."

~Bill Watterson

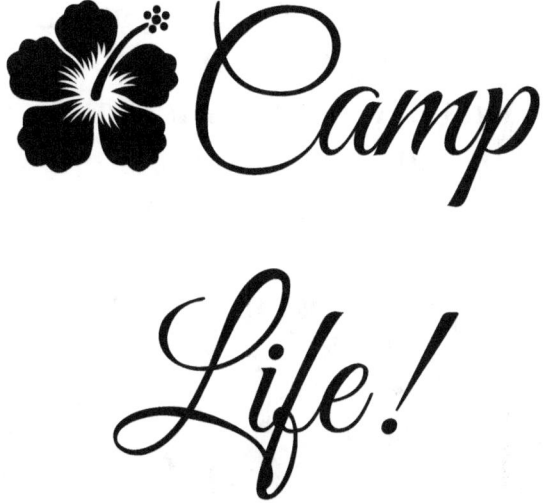

DE OPPRESSO LIBER
(Free the Oppressed)

Year by year, we seek hope's light.
Who are we in this fight?
Pawns in the humanitarian field
Day by day, distanced from justice.
This is the refugee life!

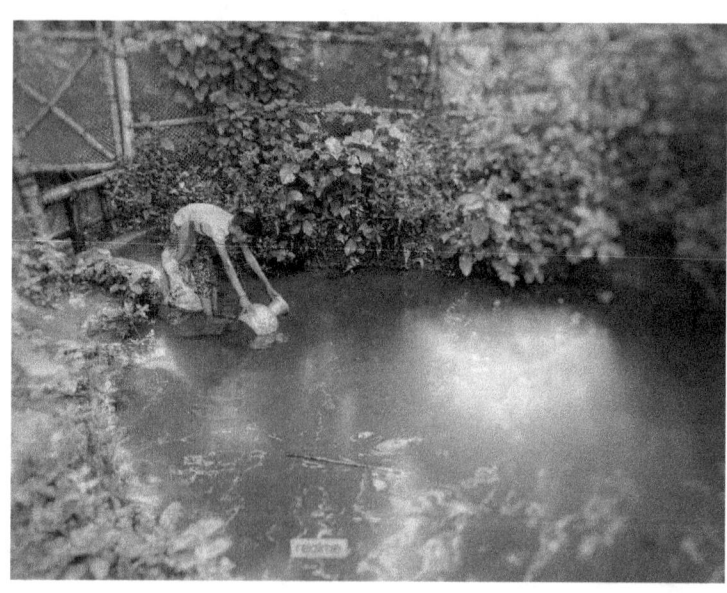

Youth servitude

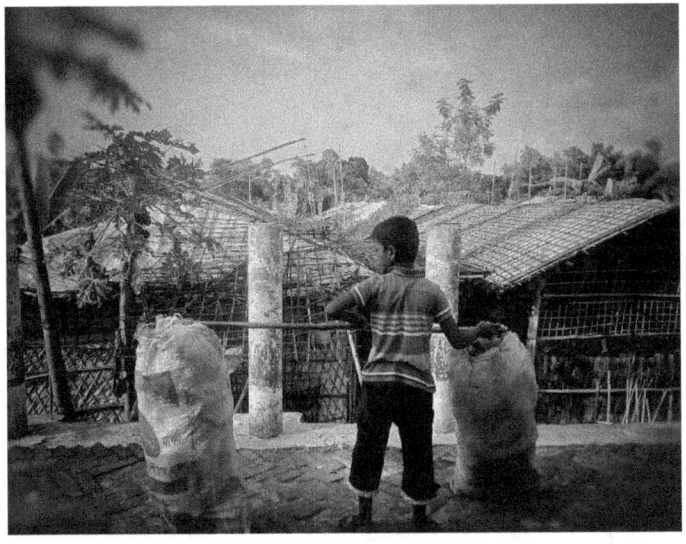

Month to month, we have no safety.
Our future looks bleak.
Hour to hour, we are away
from food rations.
Minute to minute, we are away
from basic needs.
Second to second, we are away
from good reputations.
This is the refugee life!

Robber of innocence in the marketplace of toil

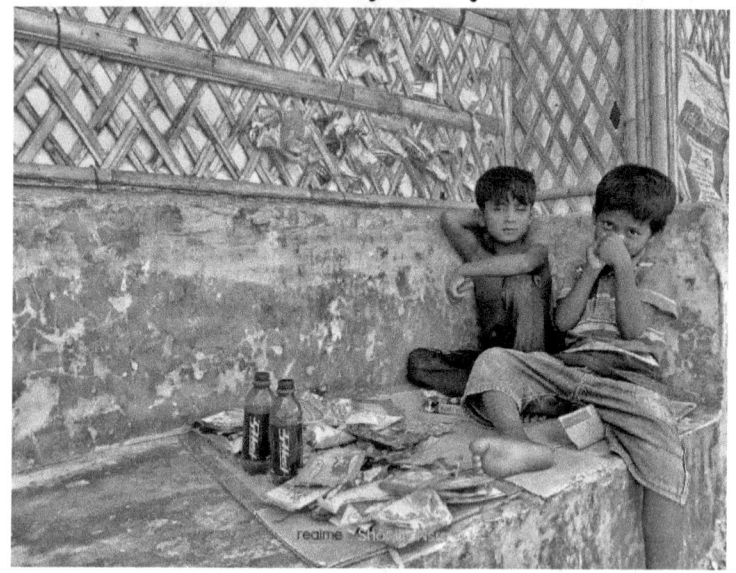

We are made by
international stakeholders.
We fail to see our homeland
and still, we are waiting
for justice with hope.
This is the refugee life!

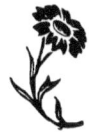

Innocence sacrificed at the altar of labor

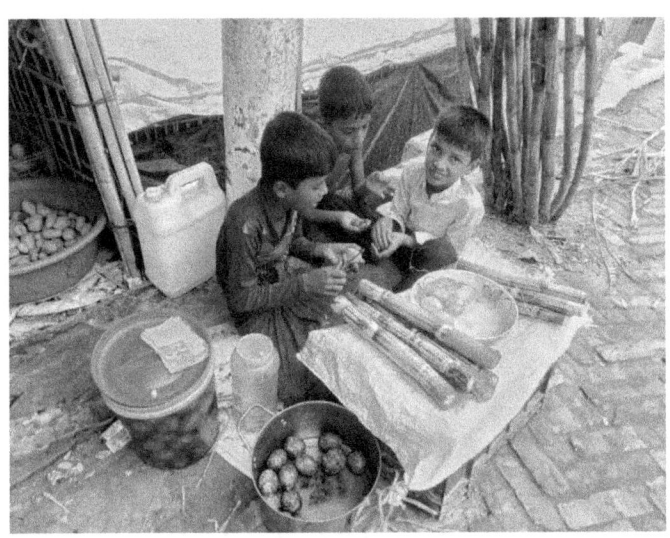

We, the helpless,
we plead to those who care.
In a world fraught with trauma, despair.
Help us! We humbly implore.
From the bottom of your hearts
Grant us the basics, we need.
Bring us peace.
Make humanity for human beings!

Juvenile exploitation

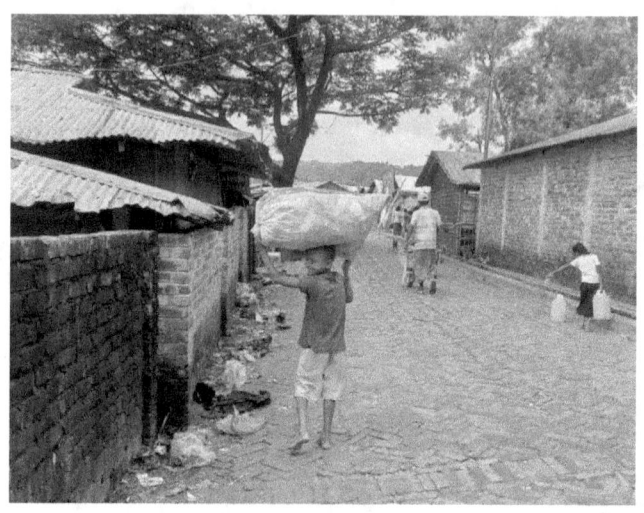

No more imprisonment,
No more pain,
No more injustice,
Bring us peace, ease our grief.
Release us from the refugee life.
Be truly humane because we
are human beings!

Child Labor, the silent thief of childhood

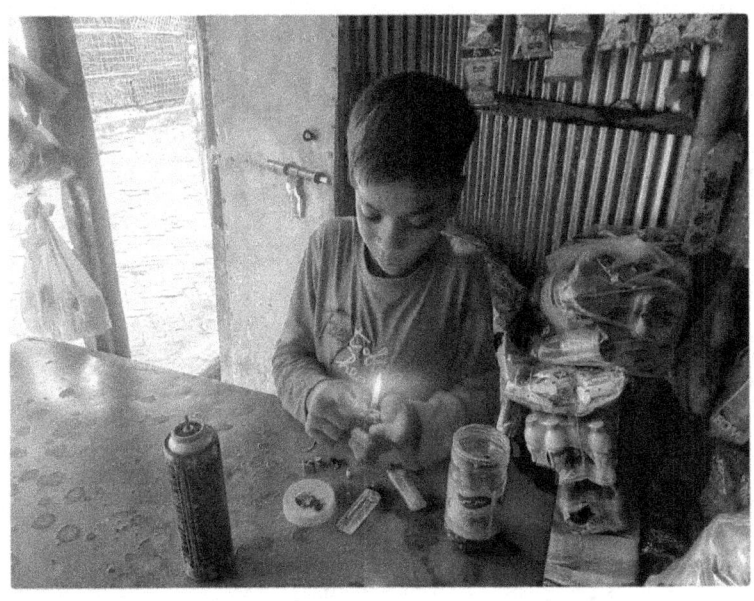

A

Rohingya boy is forced to work to provide for his family. In this photo, he is repairing a match.

Within the Rohingya community, the shadows of child labor loom ominously, particularly after the World Food Programme's reduction in food assistance.

This meager support proves insufficient to sustain the families, compelling many children to contribute to their households' income.

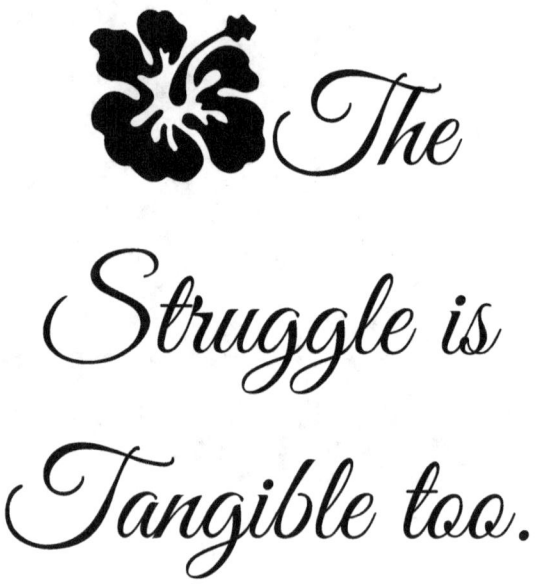

The

Struggle is

Tangible too.

Rohim Ullah

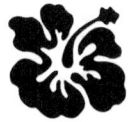

Amidst the struggles galore, he finds the strength to rise once more.

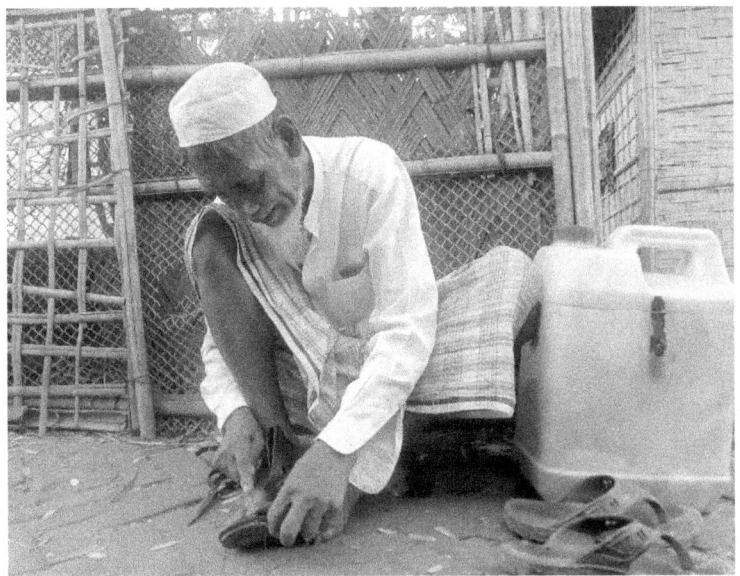

This elderly Rohingya man repairs shoes to support his family.

Coaxing water from the
depths of the tubwell.
Innocence shines and
rings out like a bell.

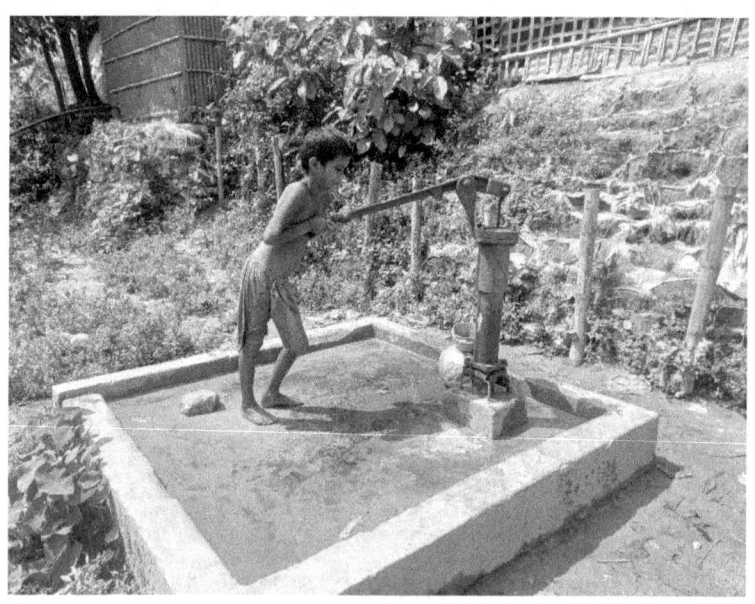

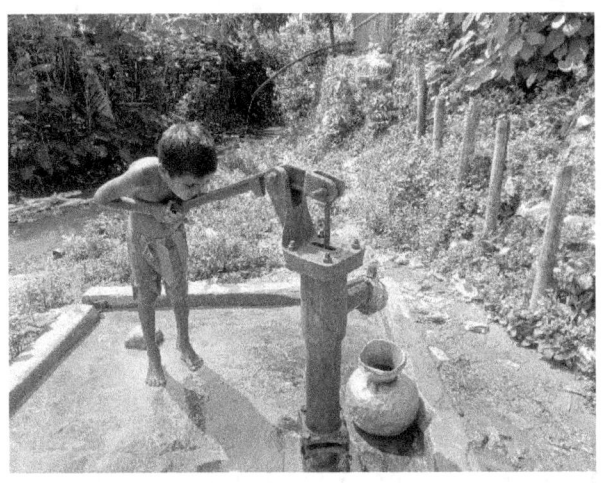

"Jt is during the hard times when the 'hero' within us is revealed." ~Bob Riley

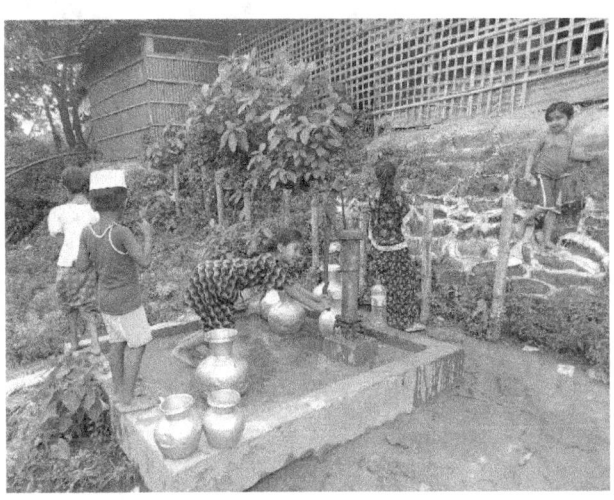

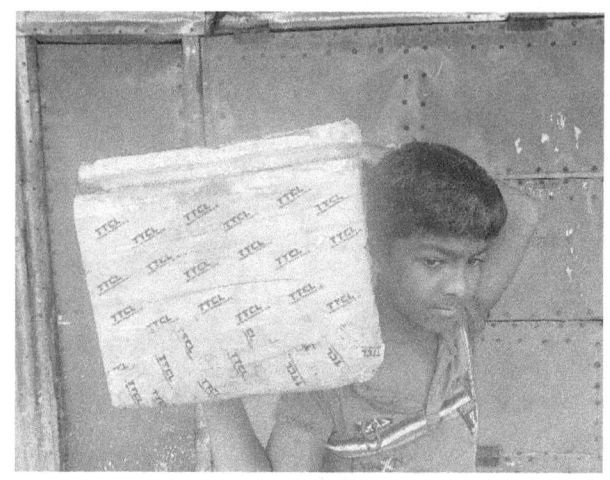

Selling ice-cream, a childhood dream.
But all is really not as it may seem.

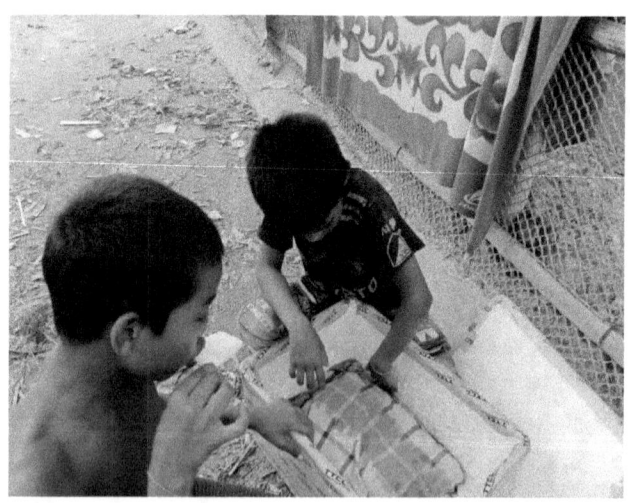

With fear!

With sadness!

With doubt!

With tears!

With hopelessness!

Without future

and dreamless!

Child Labor

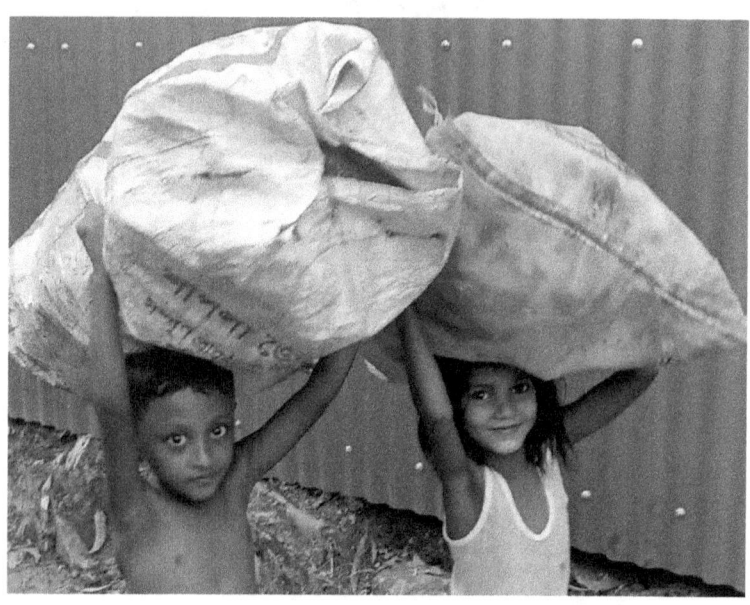

It's a horrible, terrible crime.

It robs children of innocence, their playtime.

Let's unite, endeavor, to be their savior

To spread awareness, to end child labor !

Child exploitation

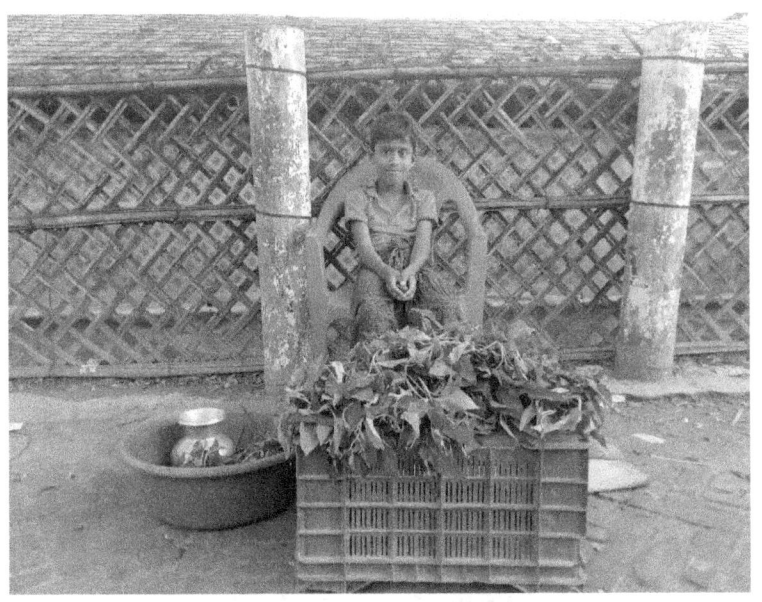

These are tales of hardship,
The world can clearly see.
To be forced into child-labor,
A truly harsh reality!

Kids in labor

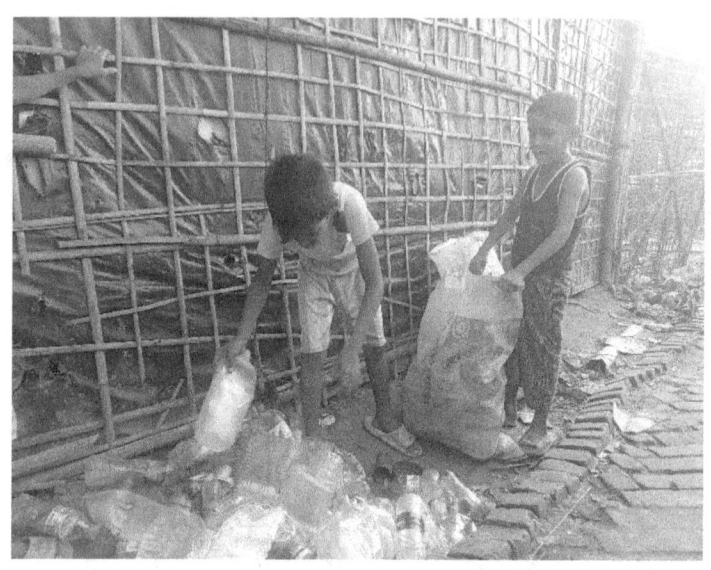

To stave off hunger,
innocence pays a cost
The plights of Rohingya
Childhood dreams, lost

Empathy

"The voice came inside his own head, and though it was very gentle, it startled him so much that he faltered and stumbled in the air. "Don't be harsh on them, Fletcher Seagull. In casting you out, the other gulls have only hurt themselves, and one day they will know this, and one day they will see what you see."

~ Richard Bach

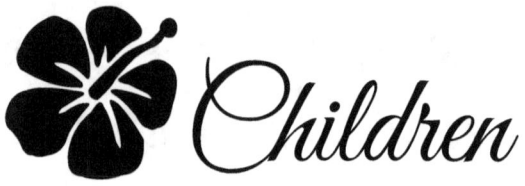

of

Myanmar

Living in a refugee camp is like living as a caged bird ~Rohim Ullah

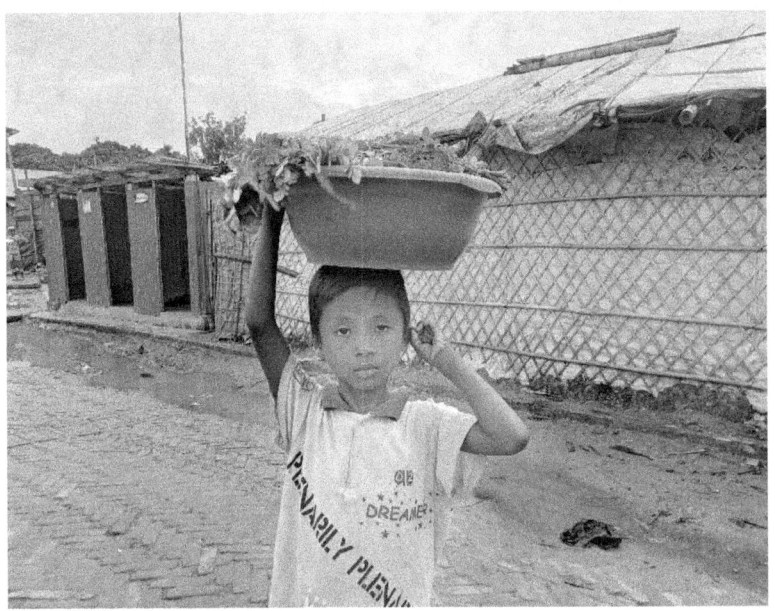

The stolen dreams of youth.

Rohingya children gathering spinach for their family

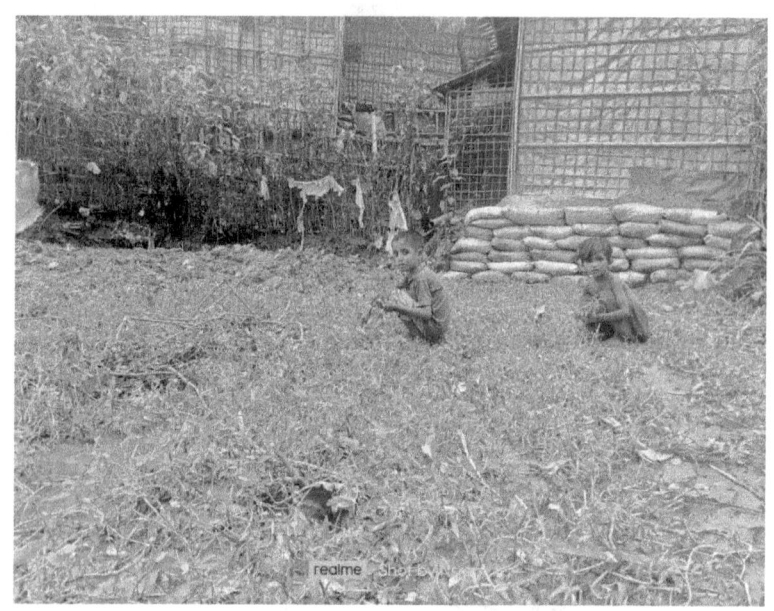

Harvesting green dreams, their story of strength, untold.

Transformation

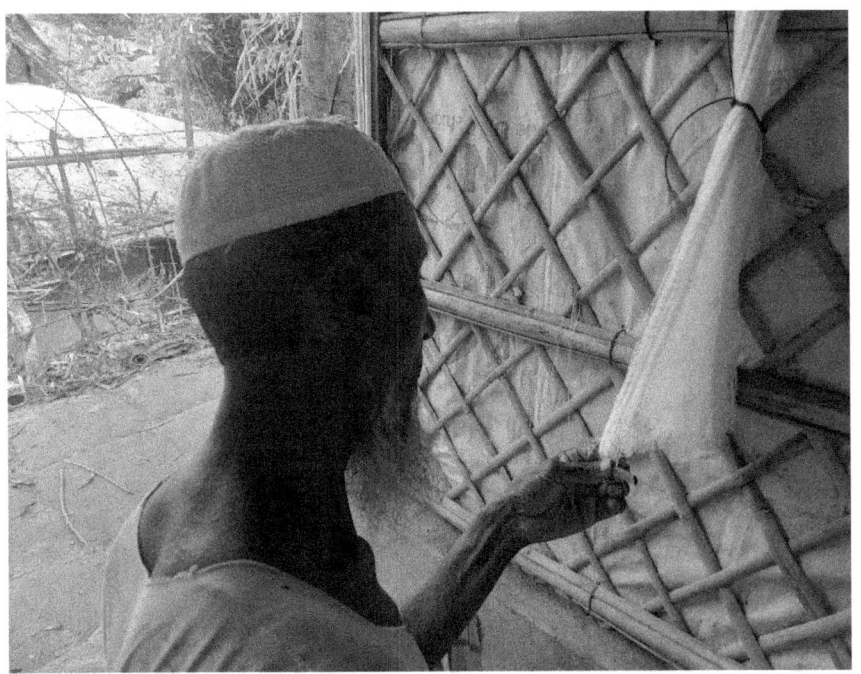

Our scars can destroy us, even after the physical wounds have healed. But if we survive them, they can transform us. ~Batman (movie)

Dare to Dream

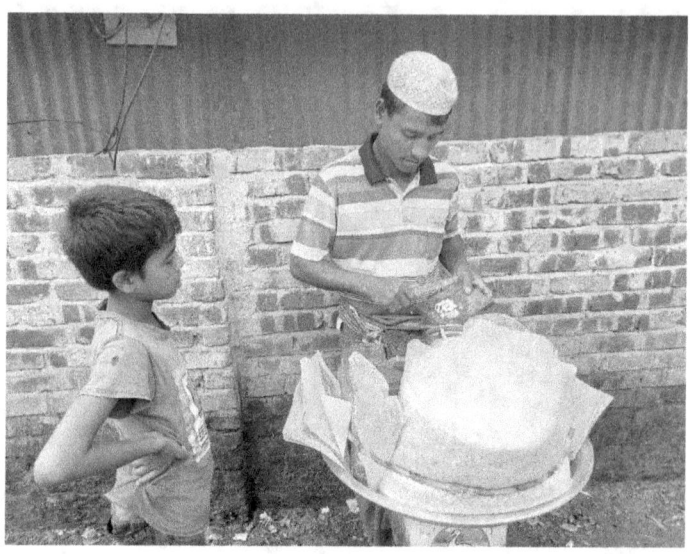

"Risk more than others think is safe. Care than others think is wise. Dream more than others think is practical. Expect more than others think is possible."
~Cadet Maxim.

Making the most of it

A Rohingya refugee repairing a Rohingya traditional fishing net by setting in his tarpaulin shelter in the Camp

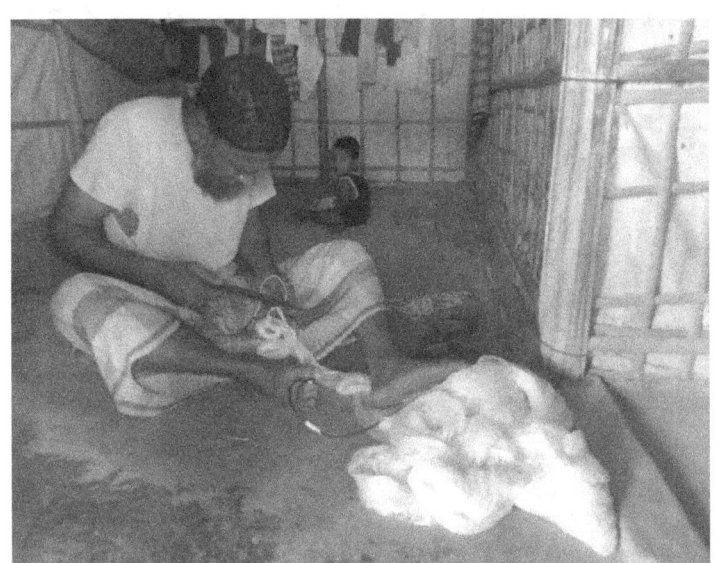

A Moment of Despair

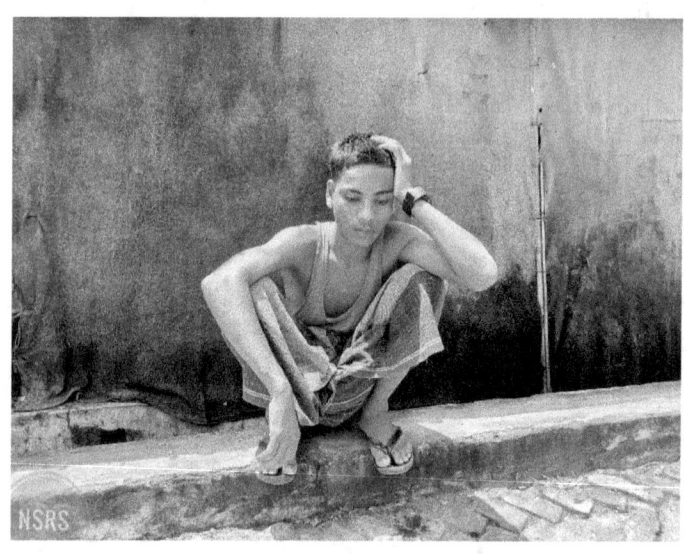

"For darkness restores what the light cannot repair." ~Joseph Brodsky

Stolen Innocence

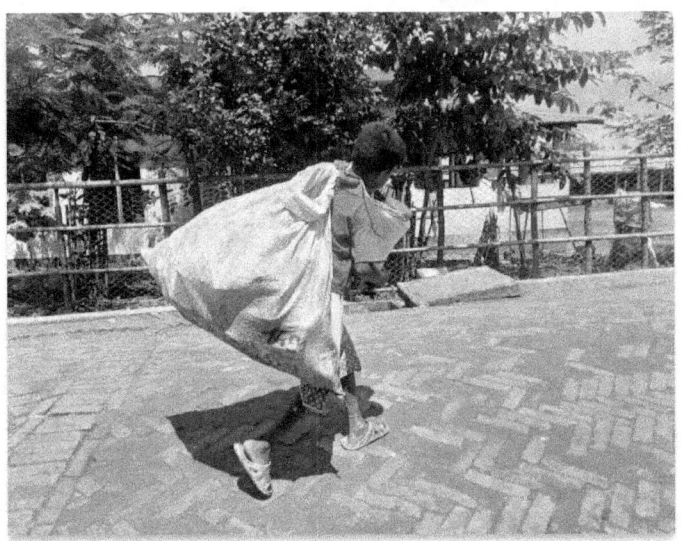

"Compassion is to look beyond your own pain, to see the pain of others."
~ Yasmin Mogahed

Navigating with resilience

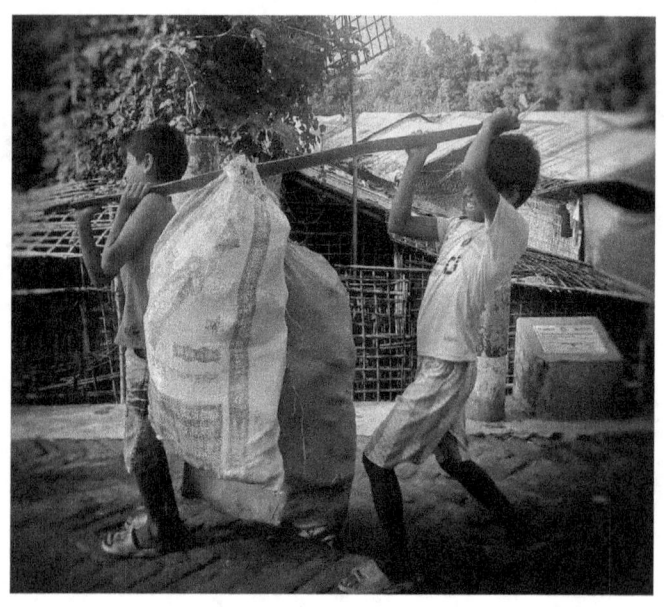

The path of toil, we tread.
In awareness, we see ahead.

Finding the silver lining

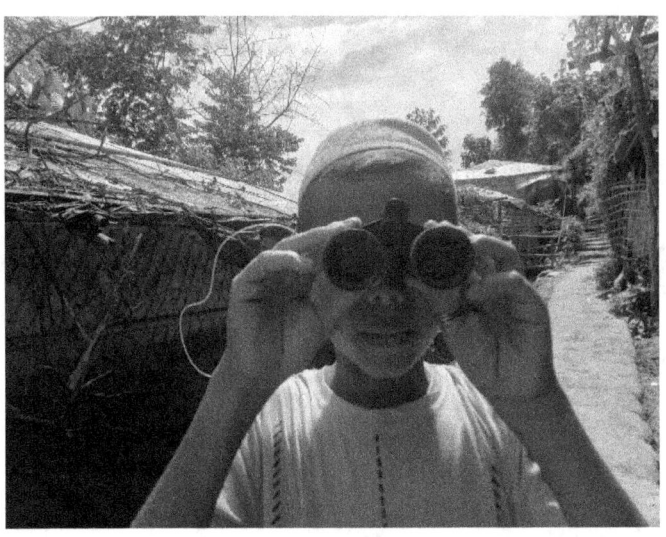

"It has been said that 80% of what people learn is visual." ~Allen Klein

Child Labor,

The Thief of childhood

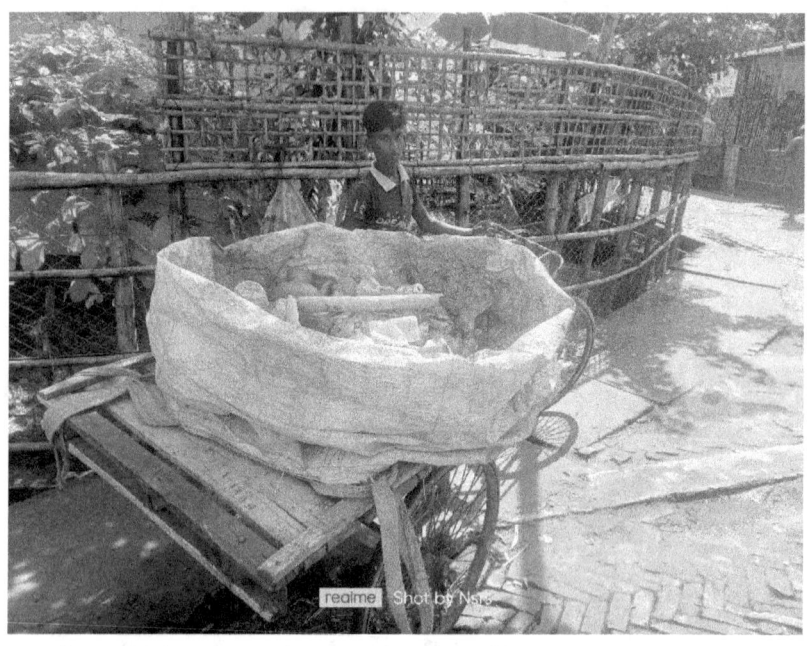

Set light to ignorance, set young hearts free!
With love, end child labor, in peace and harmony!

Weaving Dreams from Life's lemons

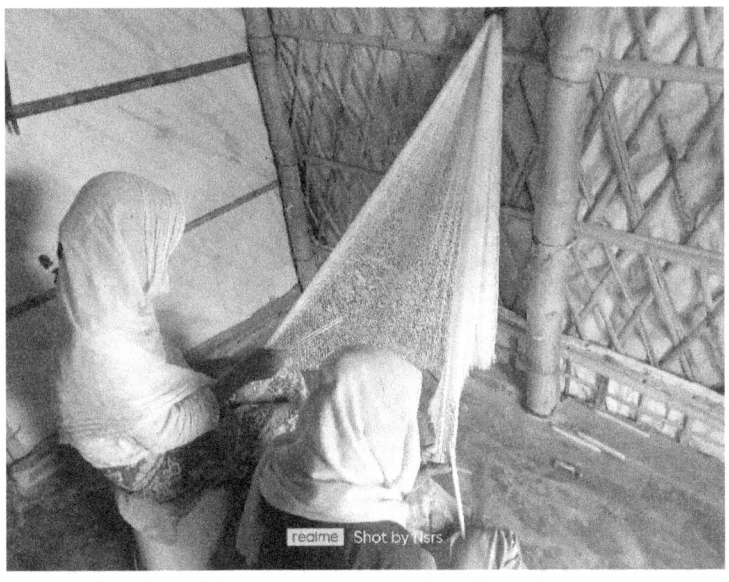

In the weaving hands of Rohingya women,
traditional fishing nets are mended, each
stitch a thread of hope, connecting them to the
sea's nurturing secrets.

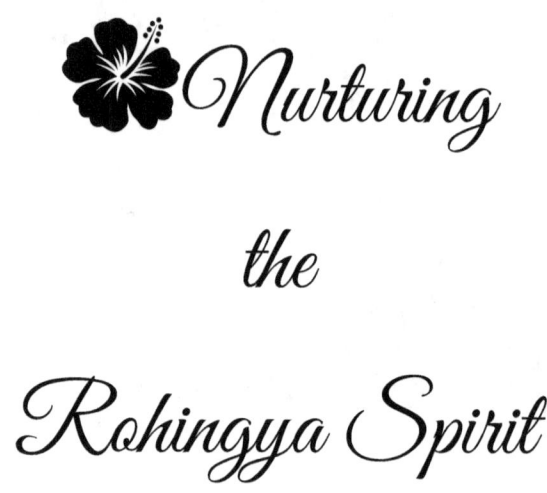

Nurturing the Rohingya Spirit

"I believe in nurturing the inner world."
~Toni Collette

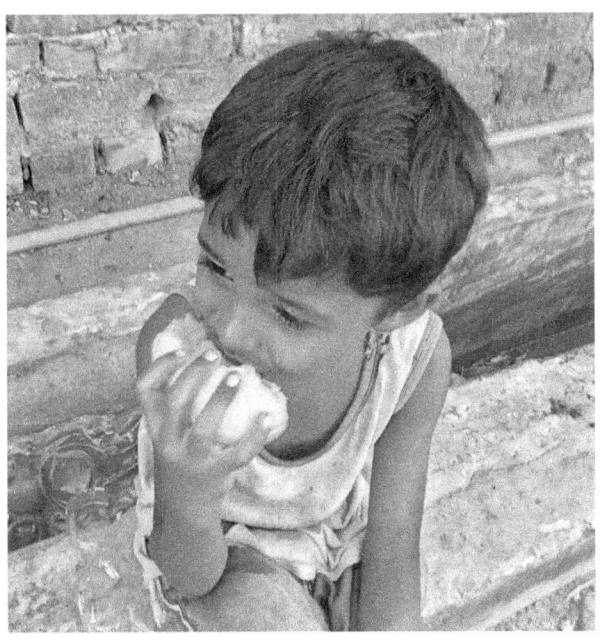

The Author strumming his guitar

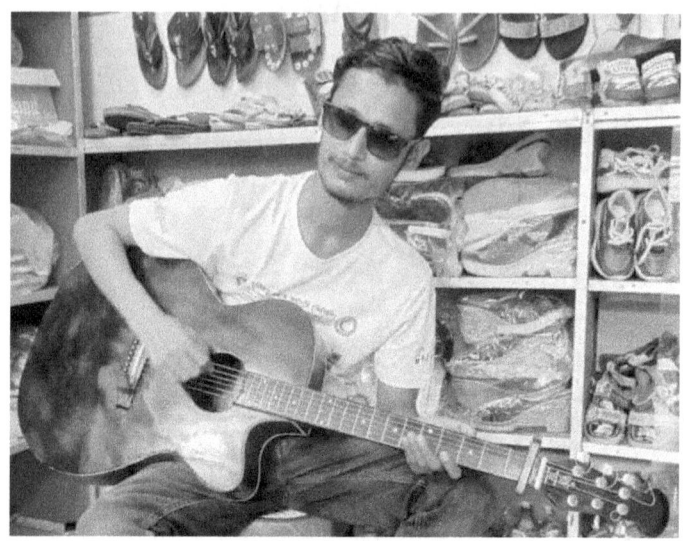

Ah dear home!
It is very difficult to forget
you from the mind!
Ah dear home!
It's so hard to feel good
when I remember you!

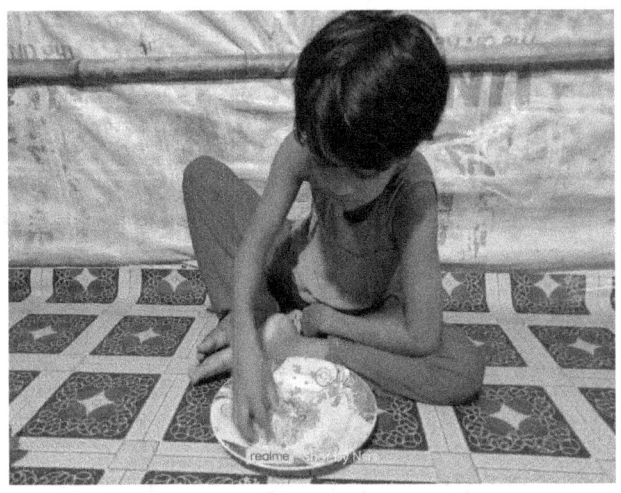

Nurture is the Sunlight that awakens the Flowers of Talent.

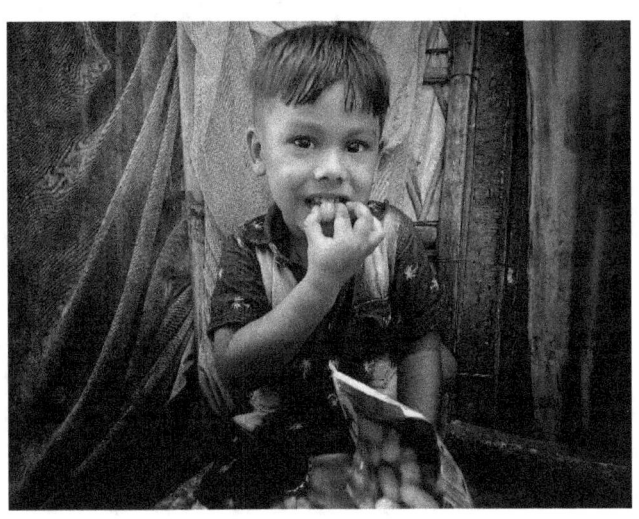

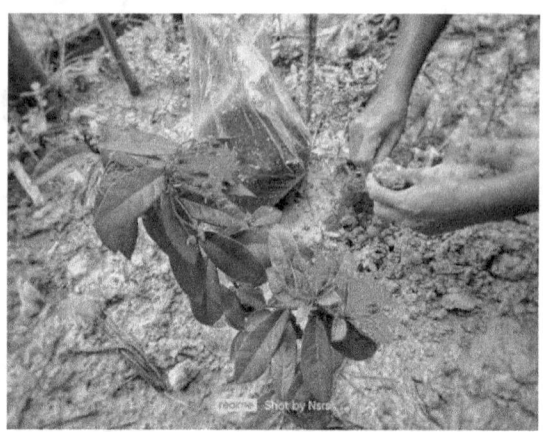

Nurturing the Soil for Day Dreams.

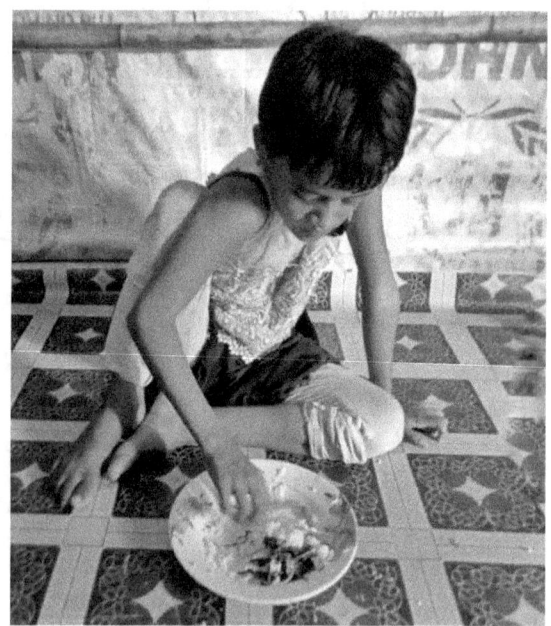

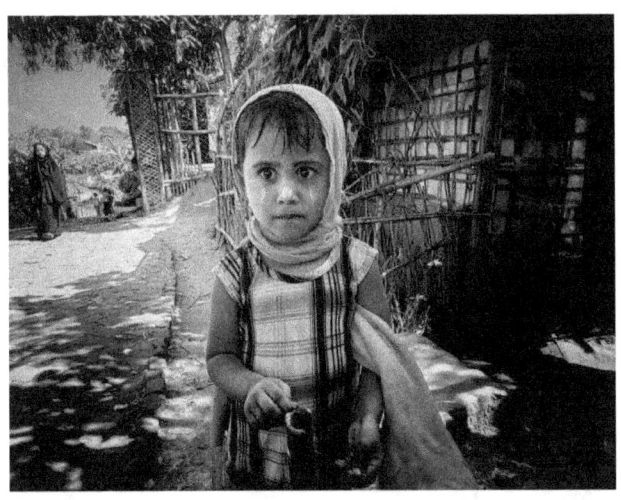

"You nurture the root, fruit will happen."
~Sadhguru

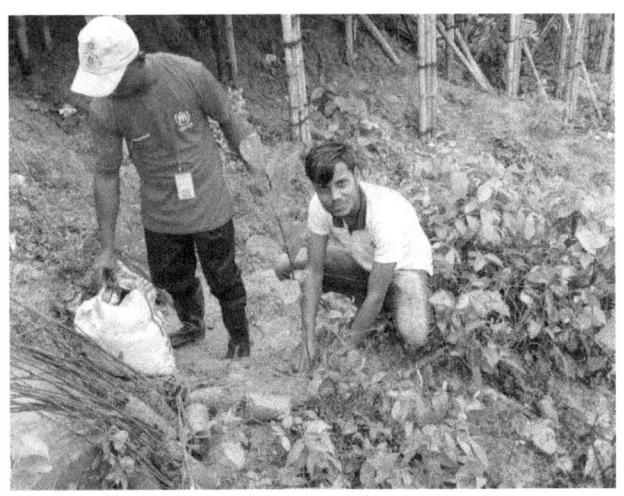

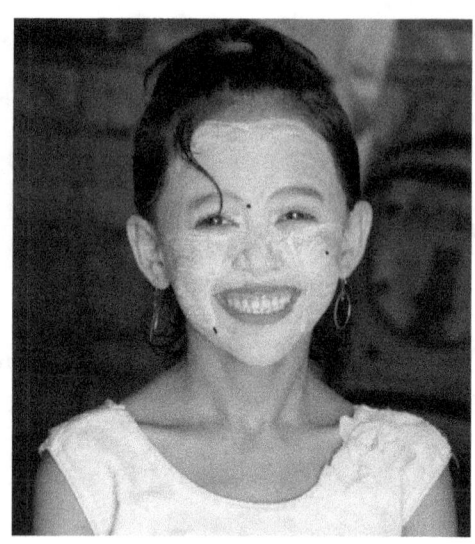

Nurturing the spirit is like tending to a delicate flame within to illuminate the path of dreams.

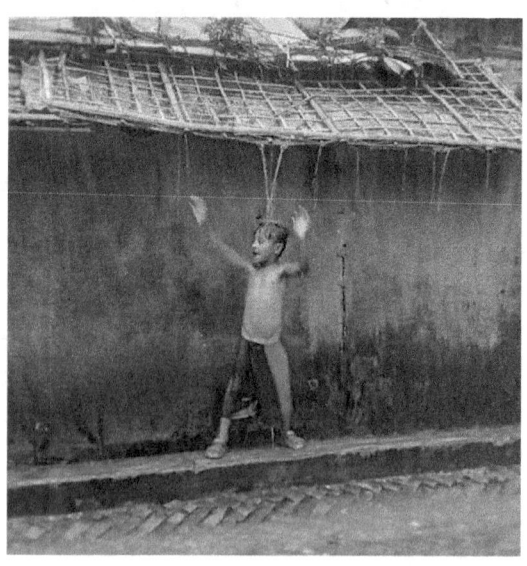

Rohim Ullah

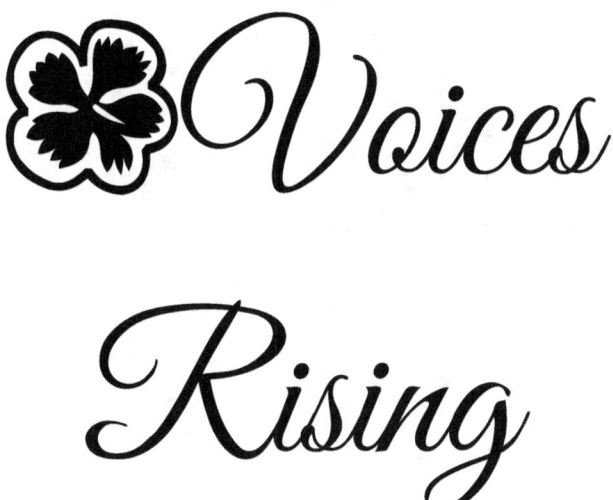

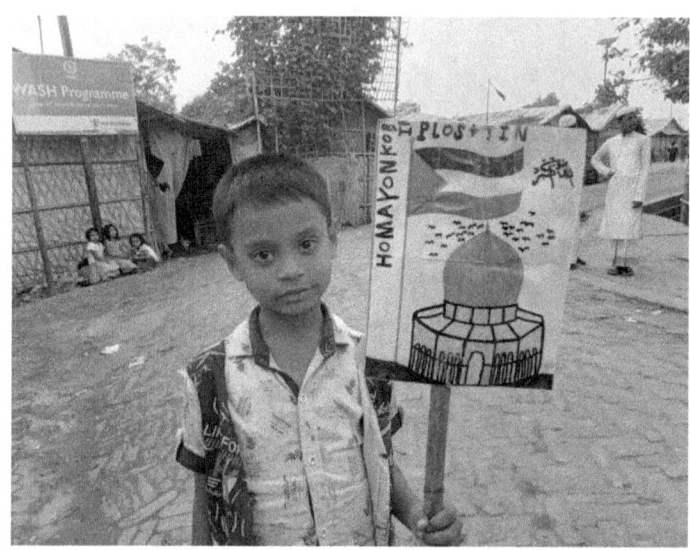 Voices no longer silenced

Standing in solidarity for Palestine.
Our persecutors crossed a delicate line!
We know their faces, even in disguise.
We are watching with vigilant eyes!

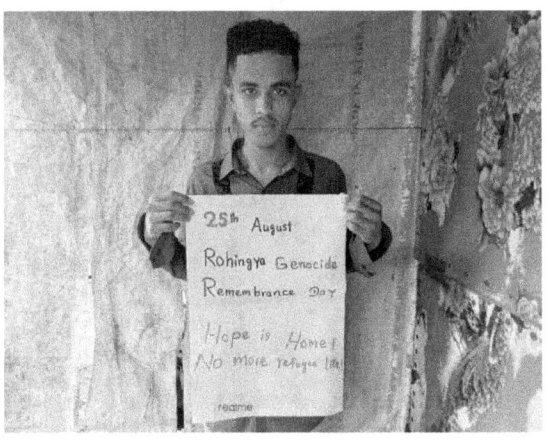

A quest for liberation, the struggle to be free.
Renewal of hopes, a new dawn to foresee.

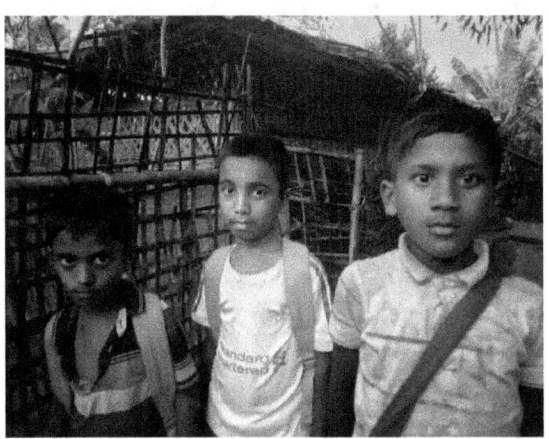

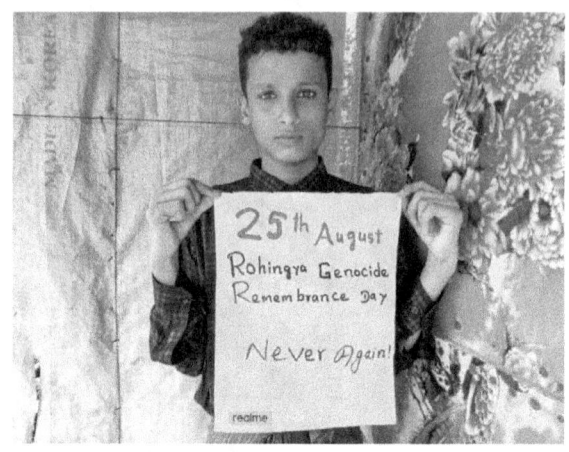

We hear the call of justice, a tomorrow's song.
With courage in our hearts, we march along.

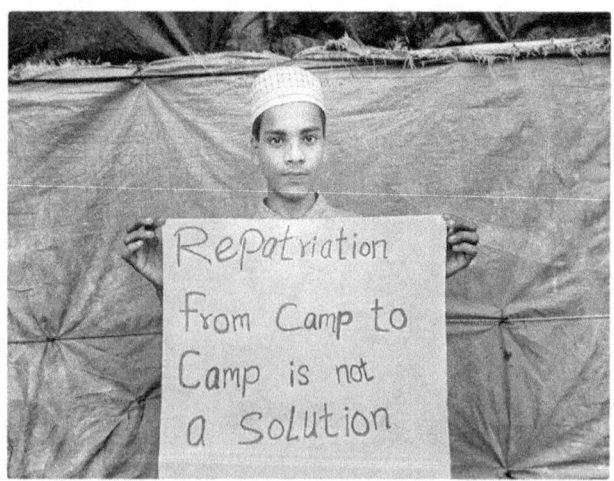

"We, the Rohingyas have spent 6 years in refugee camps in Bangladesh. We want to go back to our country Myanmar. Please don't let the world forget us because of the wars in the world." ~Fazal Ahmed

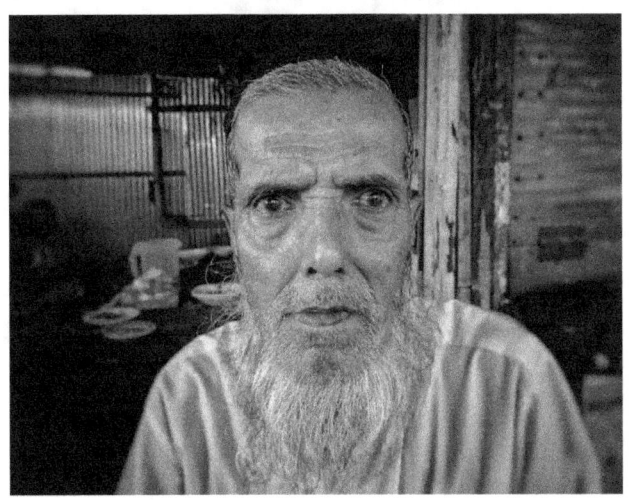

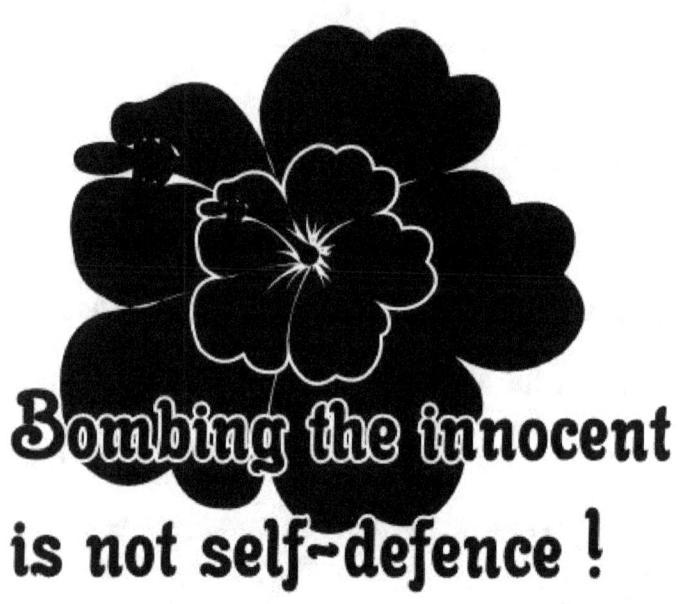

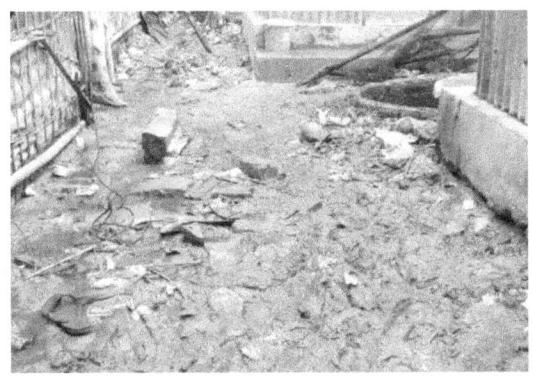

"People say that Rohingyas are dying and suffering with dengue in the refugee camps but everyone should understand that refugee camps are homes and villages of dengue." ~Rohim Ullah

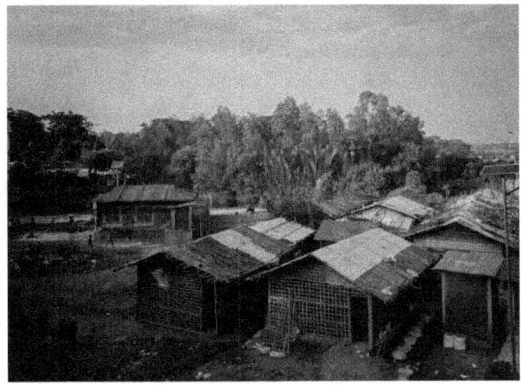

Poetic Grace

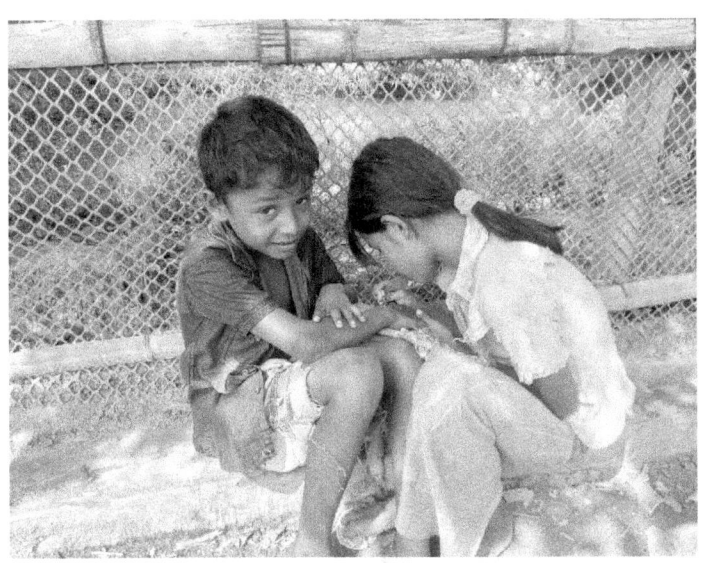

In adversity, poetic grace unfolds.
A girl paints mehendi, a story untold.
With love, her brother's hand adorned.
In these tough times, a bond reborn.

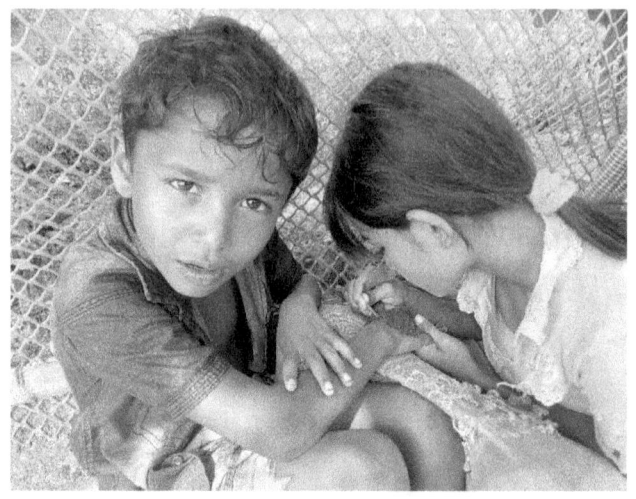

A Rohingya girl is drawing flower with
mehndi in the hand of her younger brother.

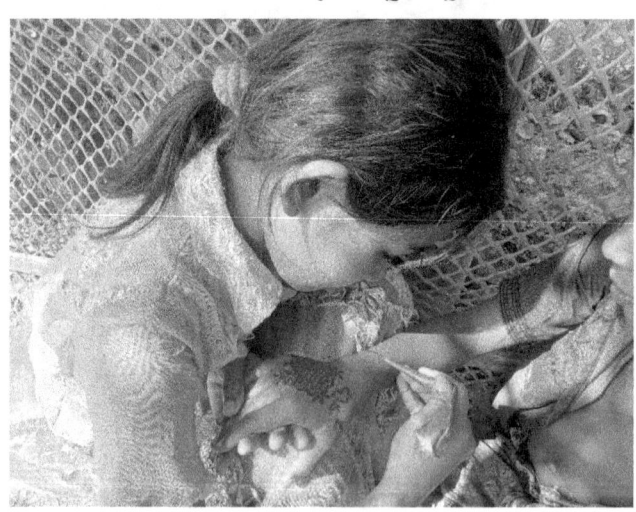

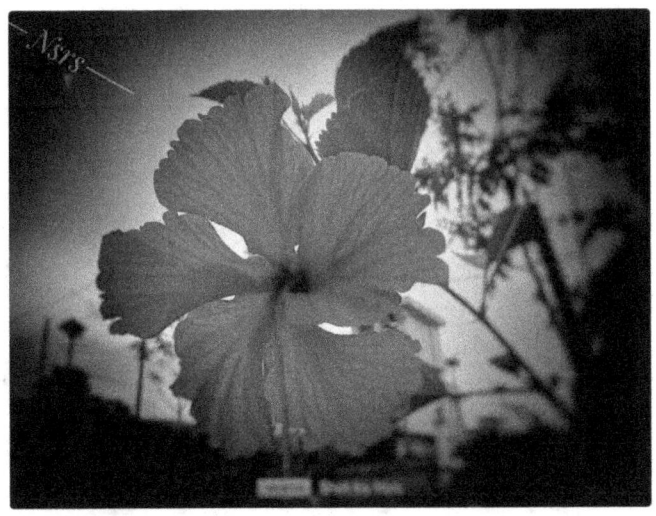

The refugee journey is a testament to the human spirit's indomitable will to thrive despite the odds.

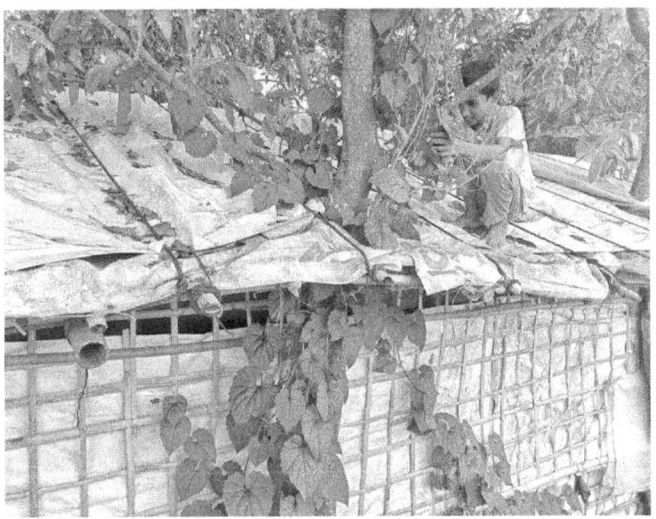

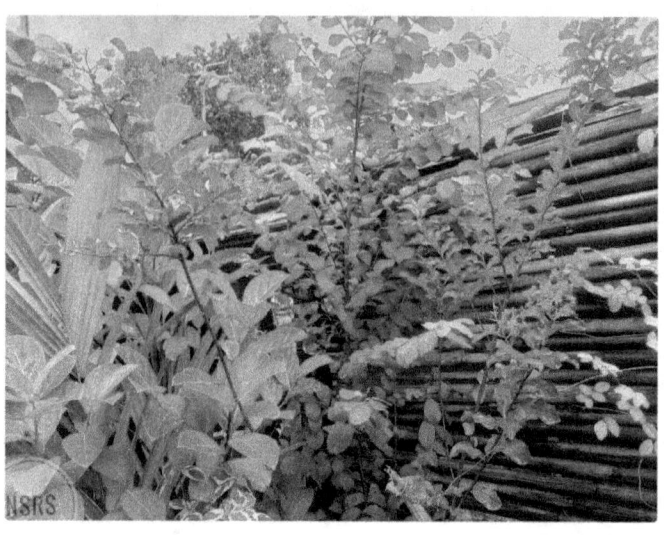

Uprooted from their homeland, they struggle to flourish in non~nurturing soil.

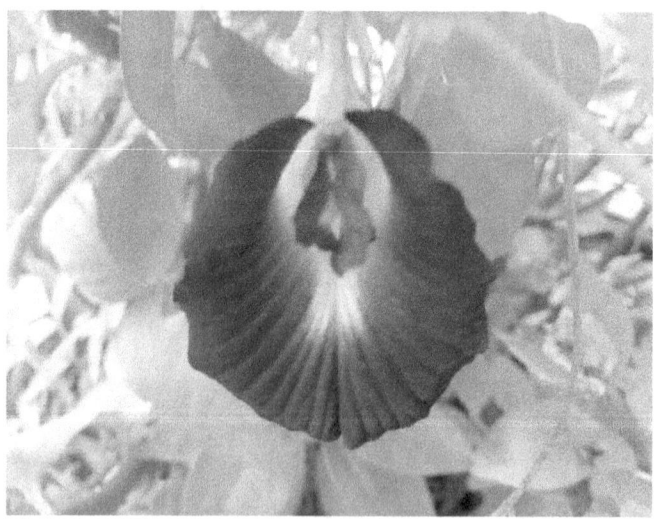

Play Time

"Do not keep children to their studies by compulsion but by play." ~Plato

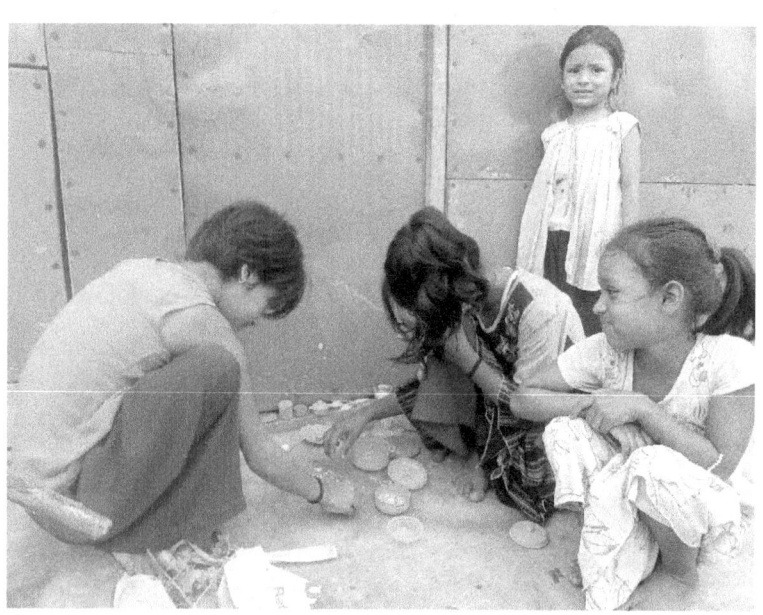

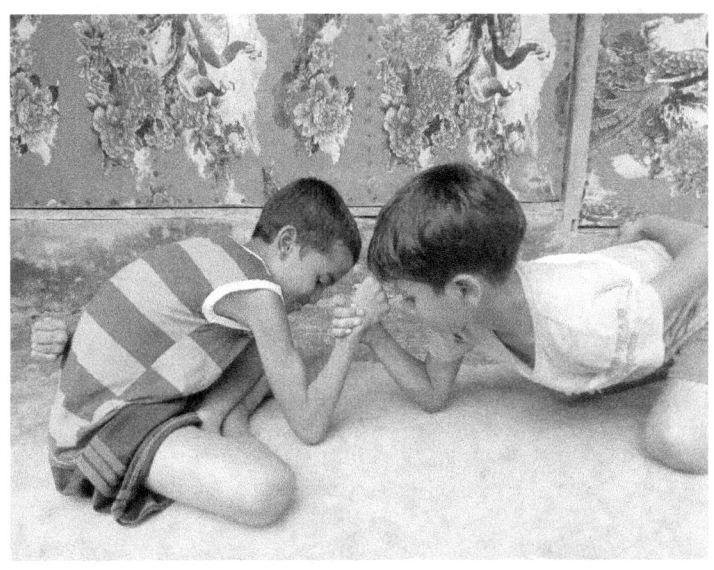

"Play is our brain's favorite way of learning."
-Diane Ackerman

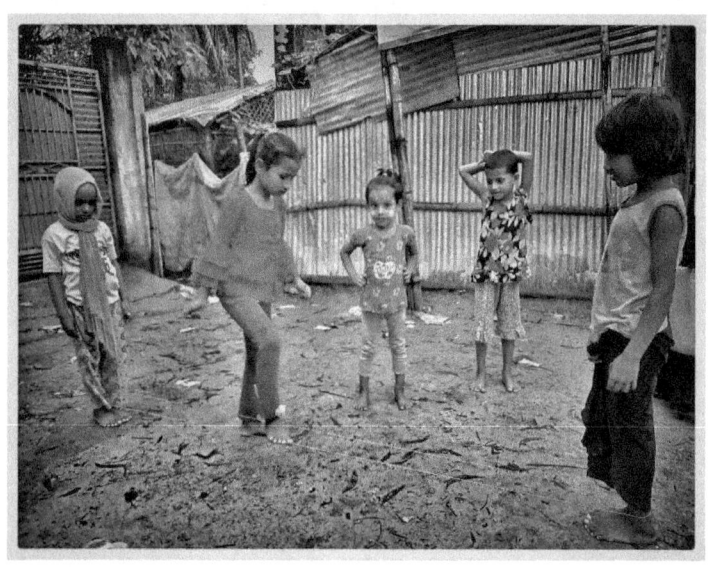

"𝒫eople tend to forget that play is serious."
~𝒟avid 𝒽ockney

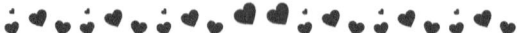

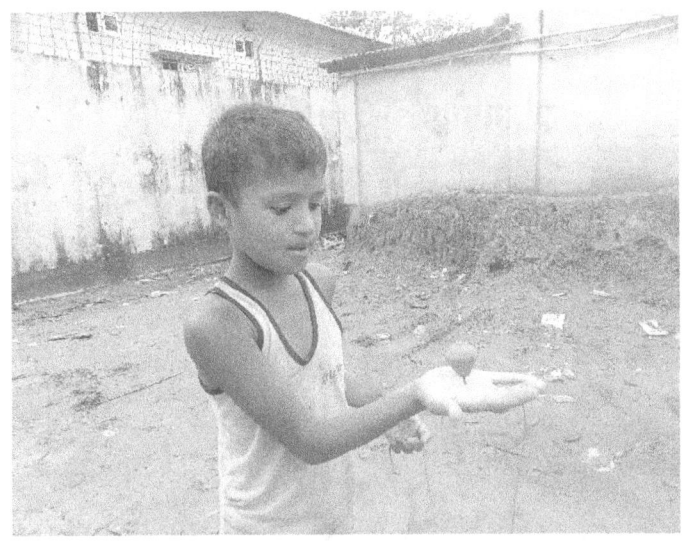

"**Whoever wants to understand much must play much.**"
-Gottfried Benn

"We are never more fully alive, more completely ourselves, or more deeply engrossed in anything than when we are playing." -Charles Schaefer

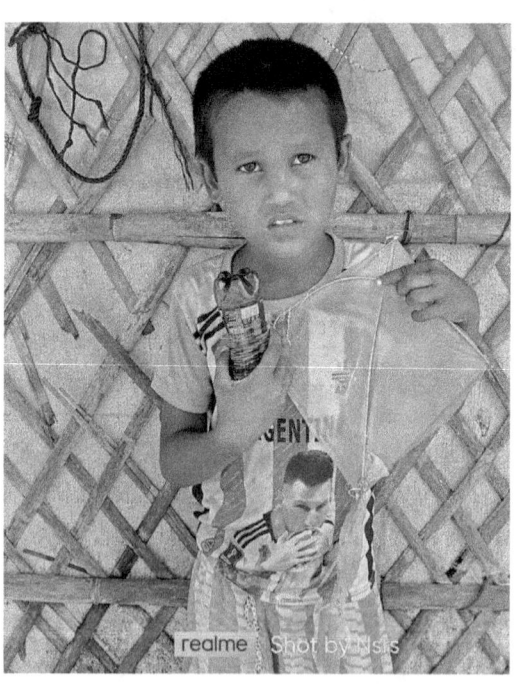

Rohim Ullah

"Play is the work of the child."
~ Maria Montessori

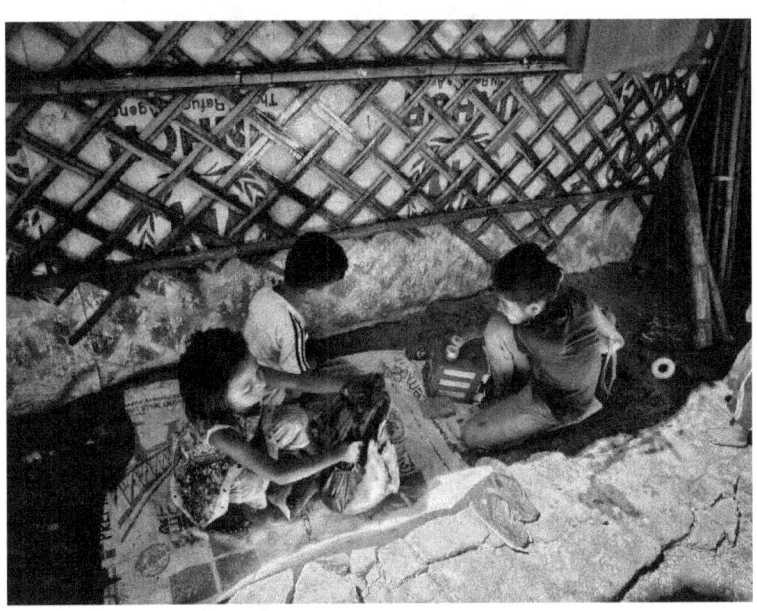

Marbles and marvels

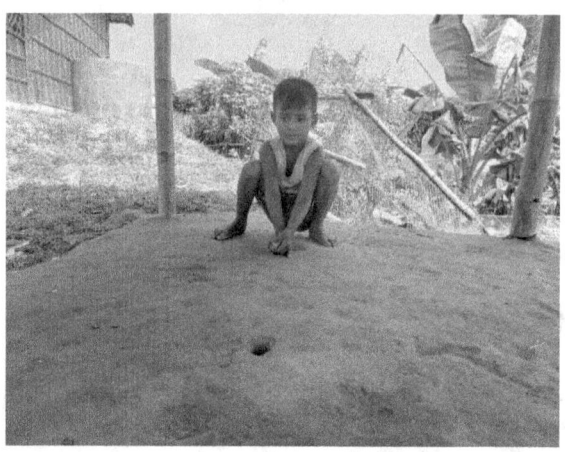

"Whoever wants to understand much must play much." ~Gottfried Benn

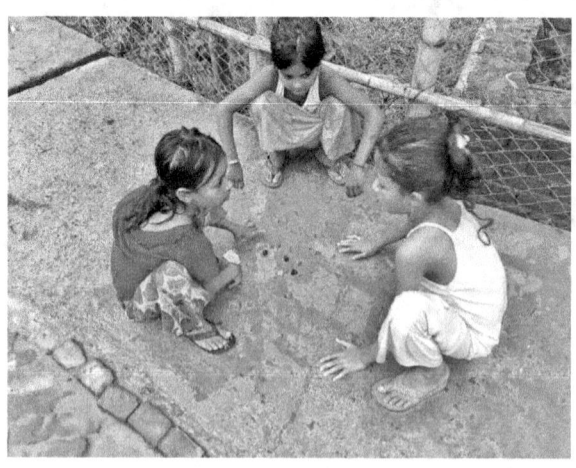

"Play is not frivolous; it is brain building."
∾ American Academy of Pediatrics

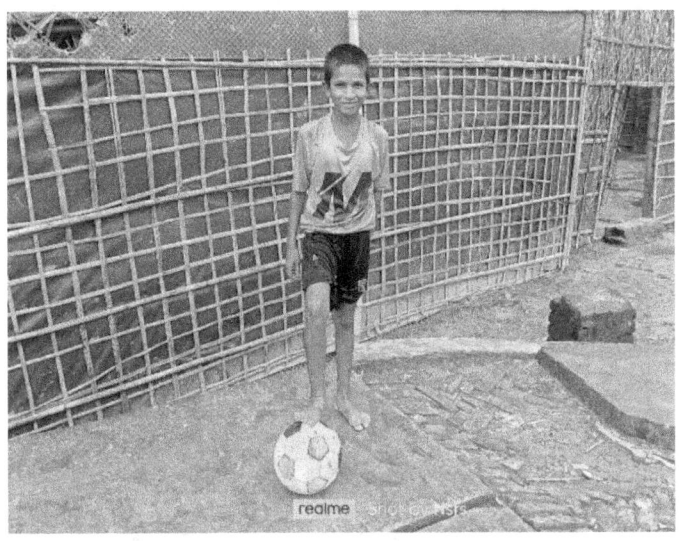

"Children learn as they play. Most importantly, in play children learn how to learn." ~O. Fred Donaldson

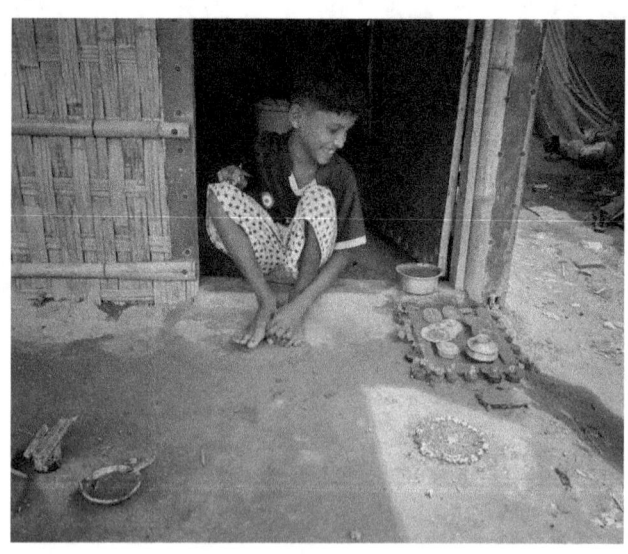

"Perhaps play would be more
respected if we called it something
like "self~motivated practice
of life skills," but that would remove
the lightheartedness from it and
thereby reduce its effectiveness.
So we are stuck with the paradox.
We must accept play's triviality in
order to realize its profundity."

~ Dr. Peter Gray

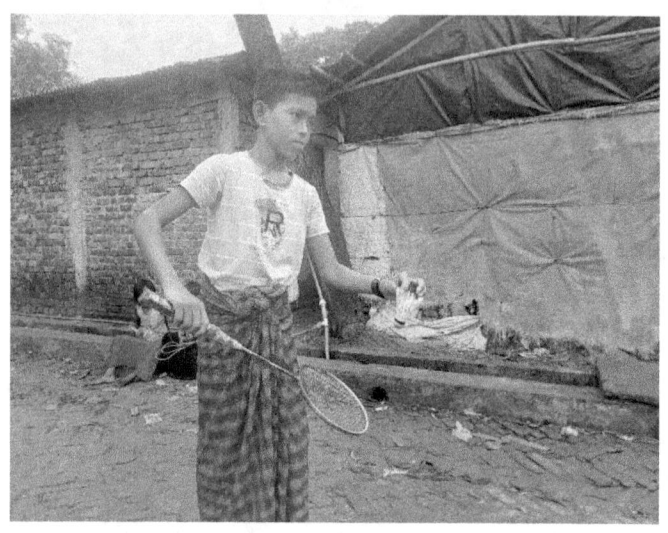

"Play is not just about having fun
but about taking risks, experimenting,
and testing boundaries."
~ American Academy of Pediatrics

A fun challenge, the slingshot wields the promise of reward in a single stone.

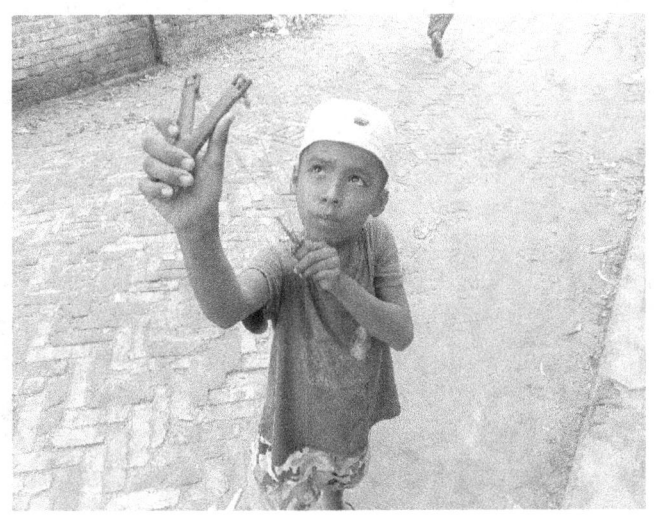

"Children need the freedom and time to play. Play is not a luxury. Play is a necessity."

~Kay Redfield Jamison

Kite flying, a dance of dreams soaring high.

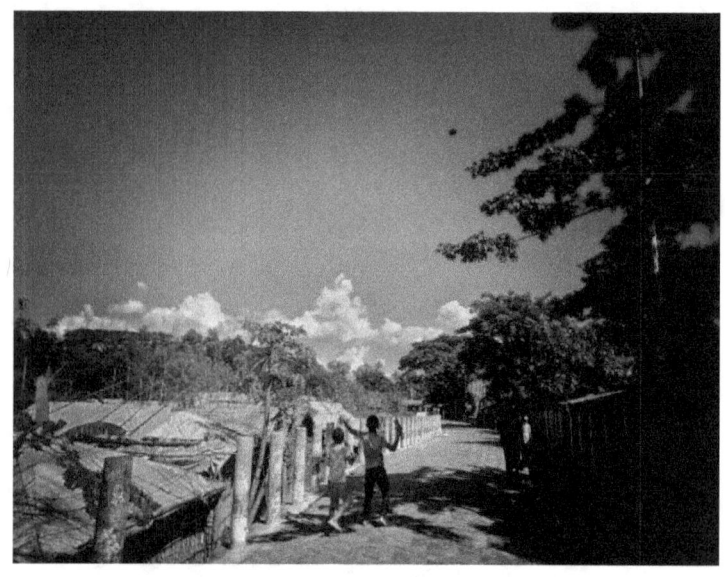

"Almost all creativity involves purposeful play."

~ Abraham Maslow

Hammock Fun

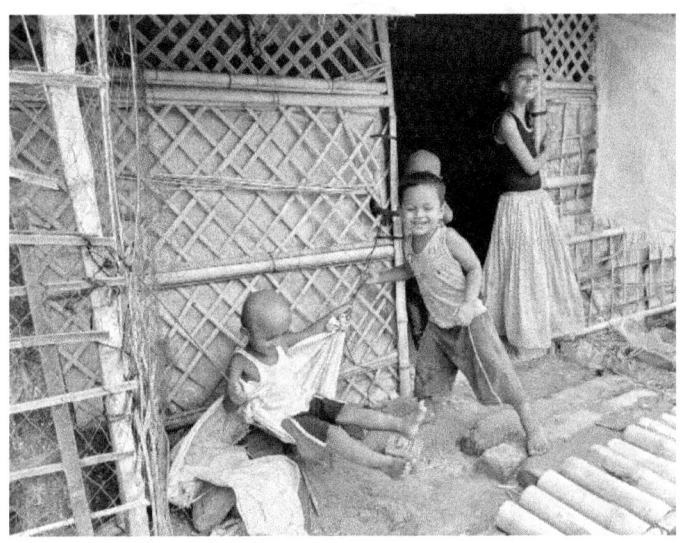

"The creation of something new is not accomplished
by the intellect but by the play instinct."
~ Carl Jung

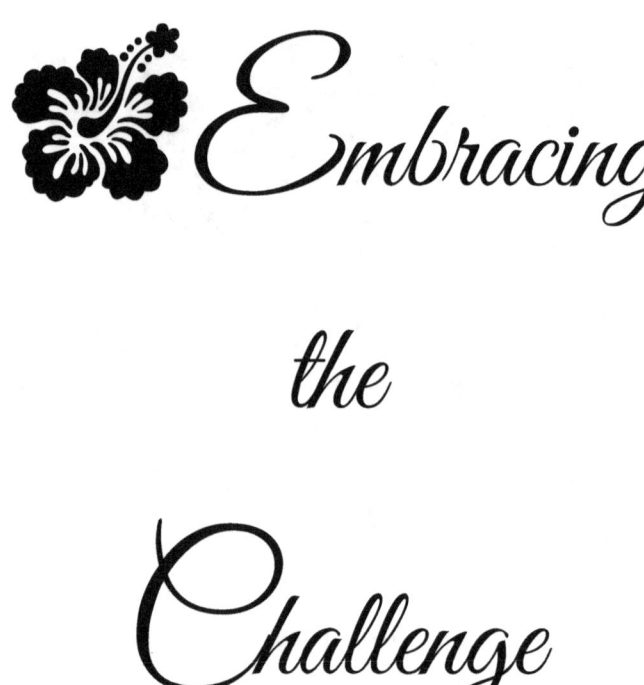

Embracing

the

Challenge

Embracing a challenge is like
hugging a rock. The weight
becomes your strength.

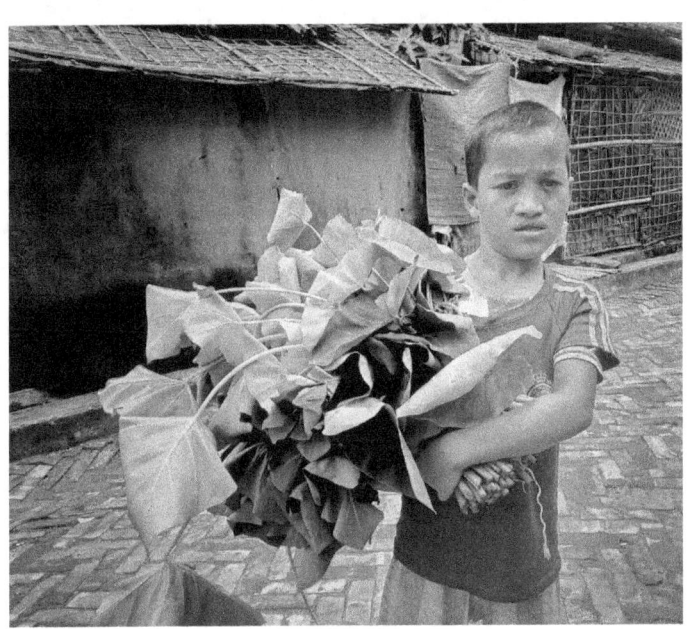

Unsafe Play Space

"Due to lack of playground, Rohingya children are playing football in a stream in heavy rain." ~Rohim Ullah

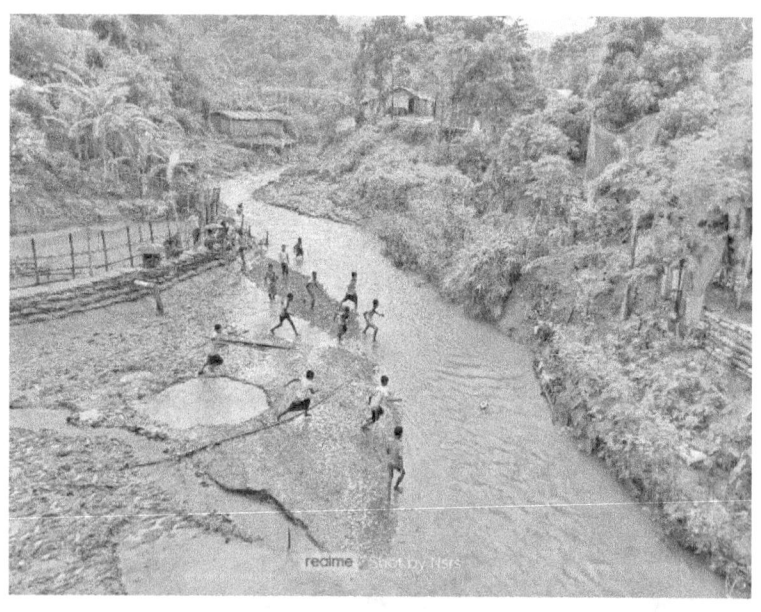

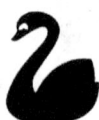

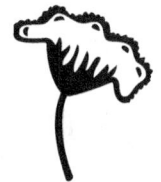

In the pits of despair, the dark, dark night.
Rohingya souls, exhausted, tired of ordeals.
This is where warriors find their inner light.
The light that can't be seen, the light we feel.

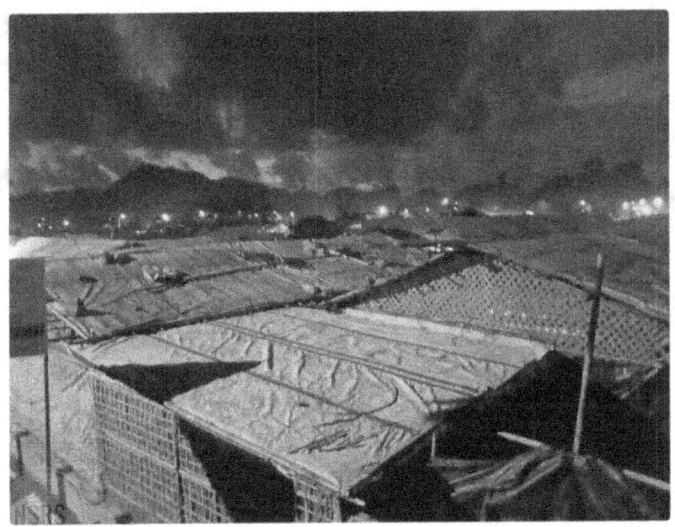

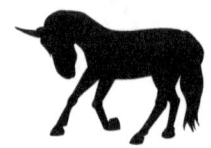

Underage workforce

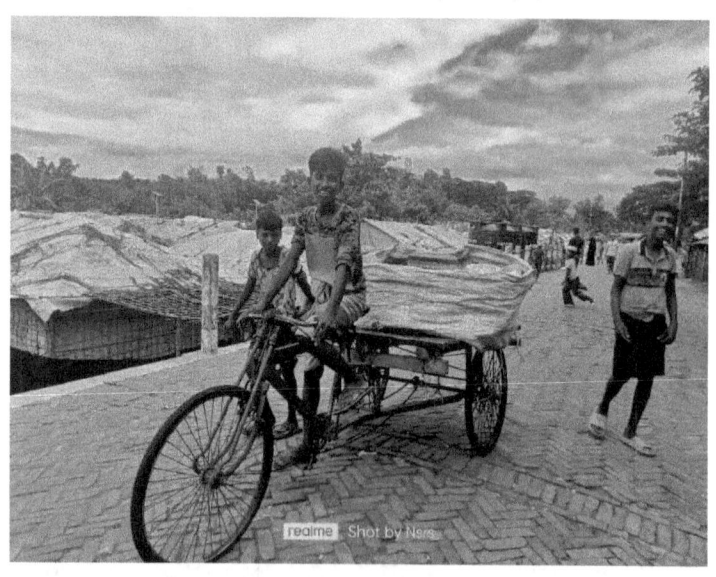

Rohim Ullah

Adapting gracefully

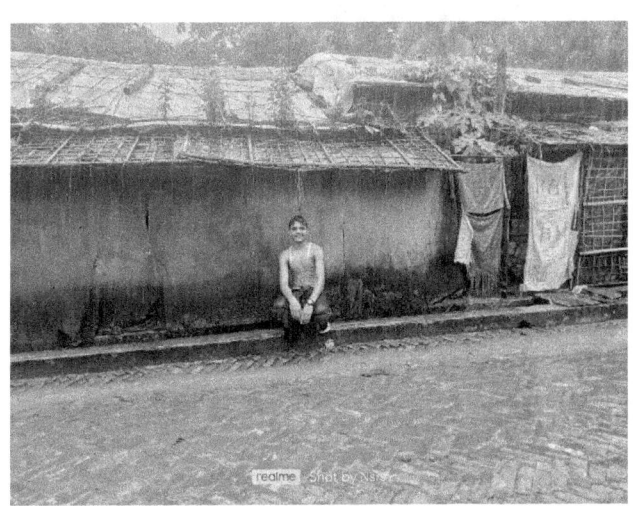

Unsanitary levels

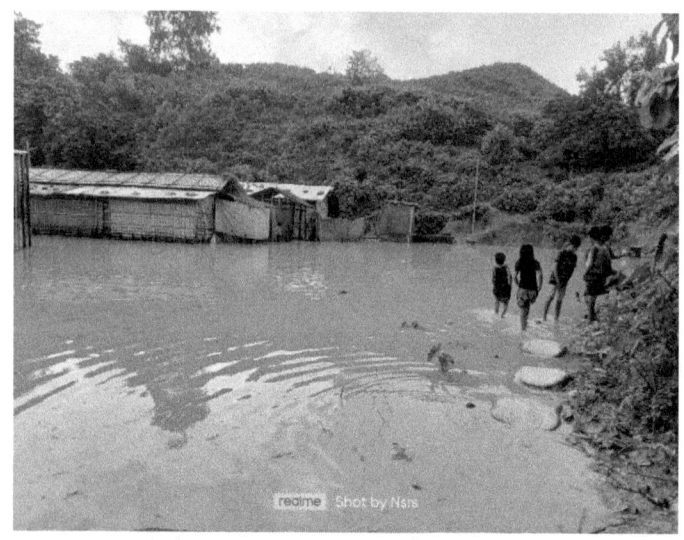

In unhygienic quarters,
they strive, in unhygienic despair.
Young minds creating a sanctuary,
For a breath of fresh air.

Heavy rain and landslide

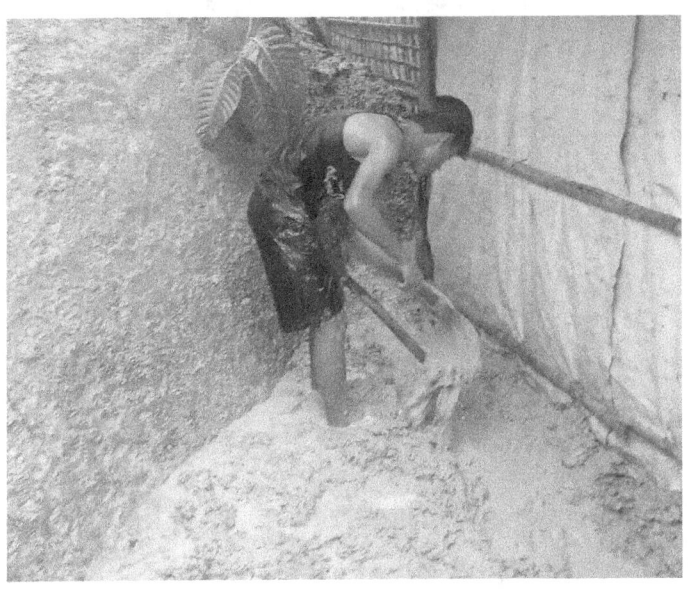

"Refugees are mothers, fathers, sisters, brothers, children, with the same hopes and ambitions as us — except that a twist of fate has bound their lives to a global refugee crisis on an unprecedented scale."
— Khaled Hosseini

Optimizing the situation

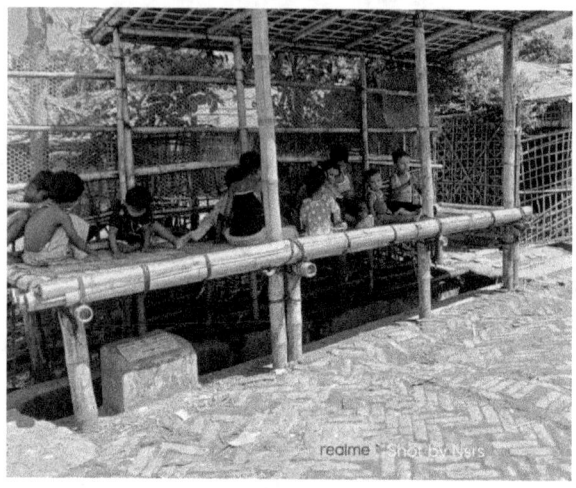

Casting hopes into the river of life, where patience is the bait, and dreams are the catch of the day.

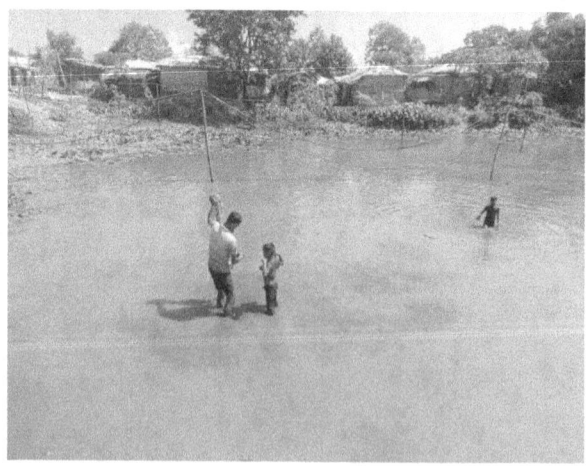

"We must see others' struggles as our own,
and their success as our success,
so we can speak to our common humanity."

~Ilhan Omar

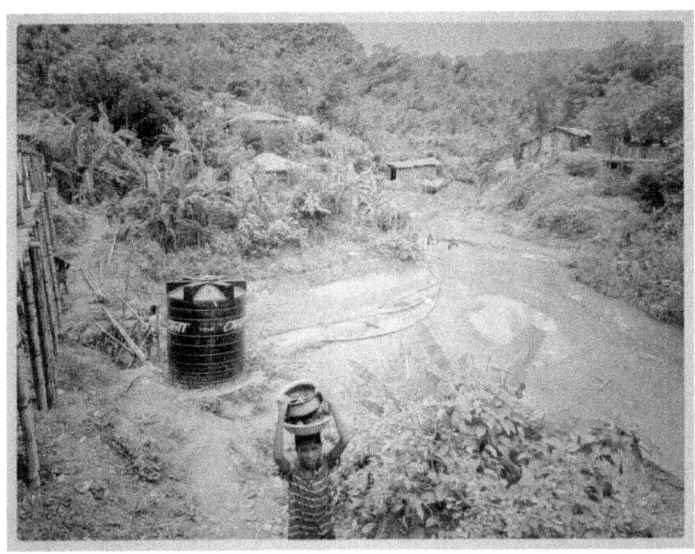

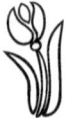

"Not everything that is faced
can be changed, but nothing can be
changed until it is faced."
~ James Baldwin

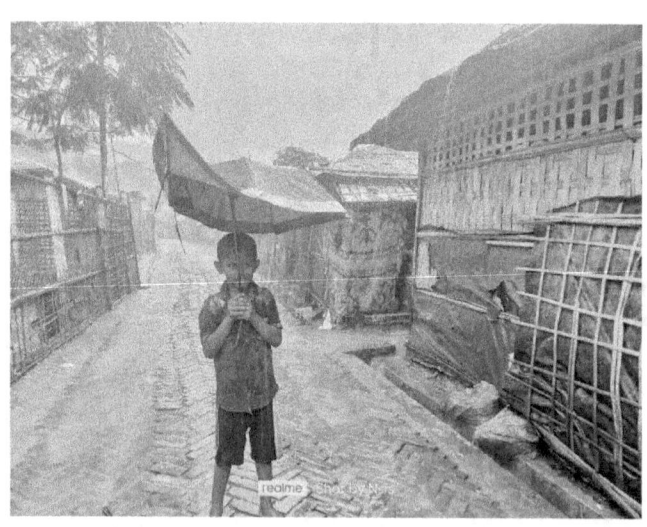

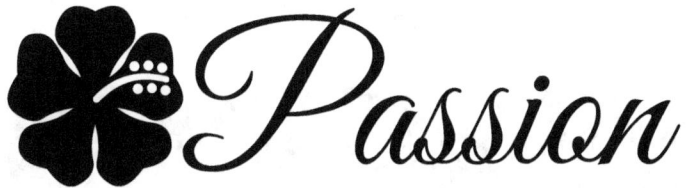

Passion

for

Wisdom

"Learning never exhausts the mind."
~Leonardo da Vinci

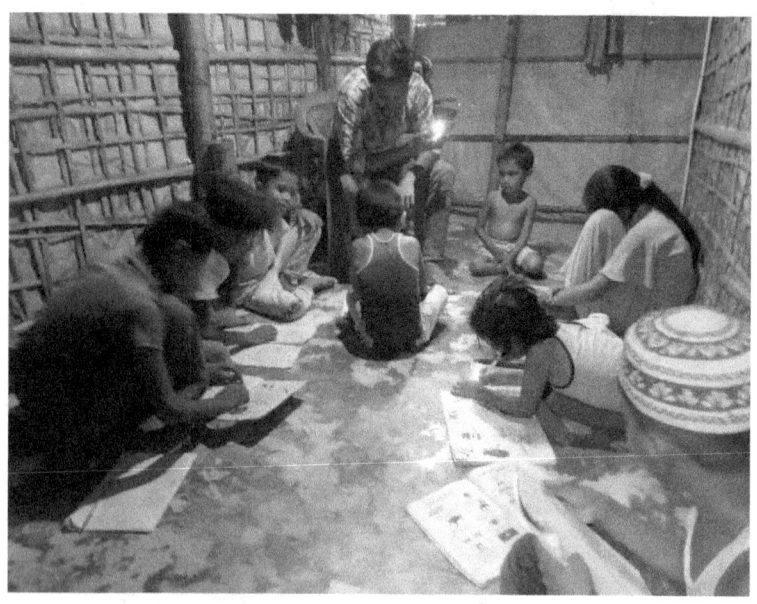

Ayub Khan teaches his students
in a Rohingya tarpaulin shelter at night

Literal Learning Grounds

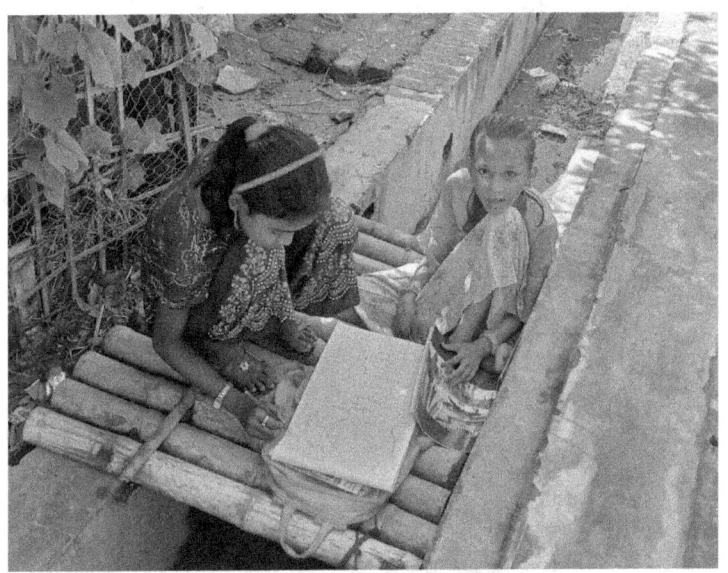

Eager hearts are in need of a place
where dreams can come true.
A haven of learning,
clean, bright, and long overdue

Beneath the moon's gentle silver light.
In a tarpaulin shelter, enshrouded by night.
A teacher imparts wisdom to hearts alight.
In the Rohingya camp, knowledge takes flight.

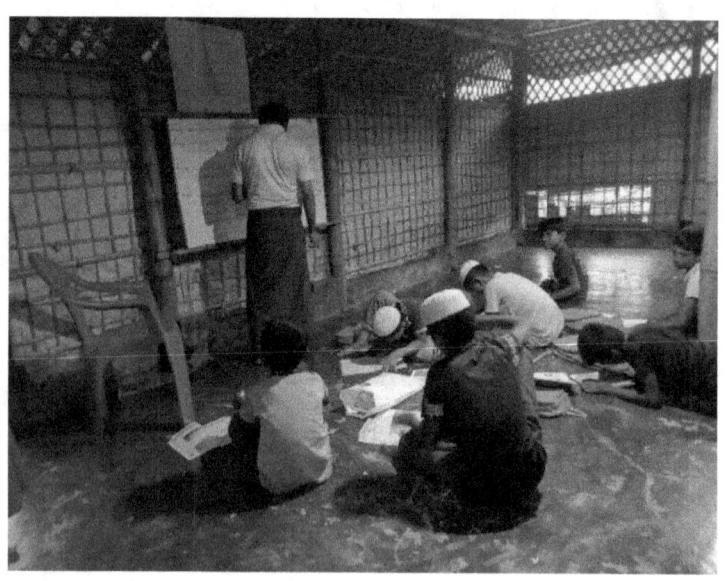

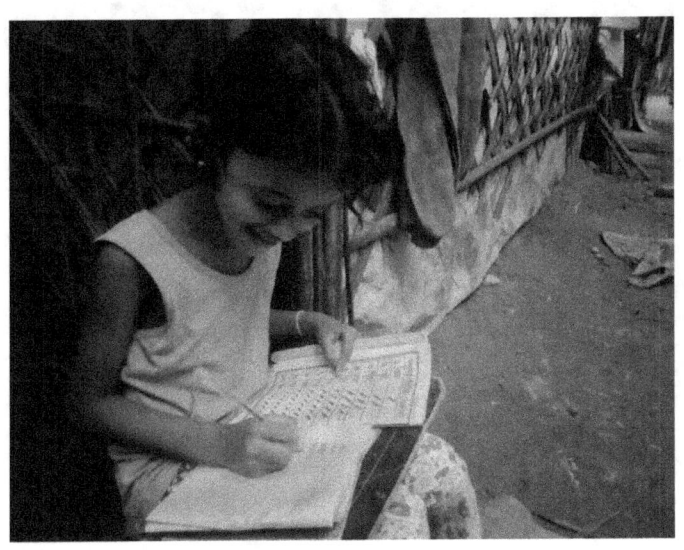

Standing in the hall of fame
And the world's gonna know your name
'Cause you burn with the brightest flame
And you'll be on the walls
of the hall of fame
~ Hall of Fame song, The Script

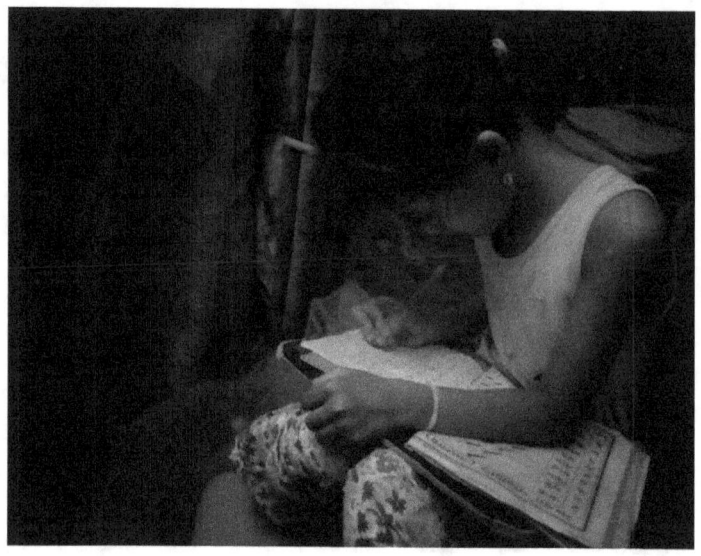

"Carry a candle in the dark, be a candle in the dark, know that you're a flame in the dark."
~Ivan Illich

"Every student has something to offer, and every student deserves a nurturing learning environment."
~ Ilhan Omar

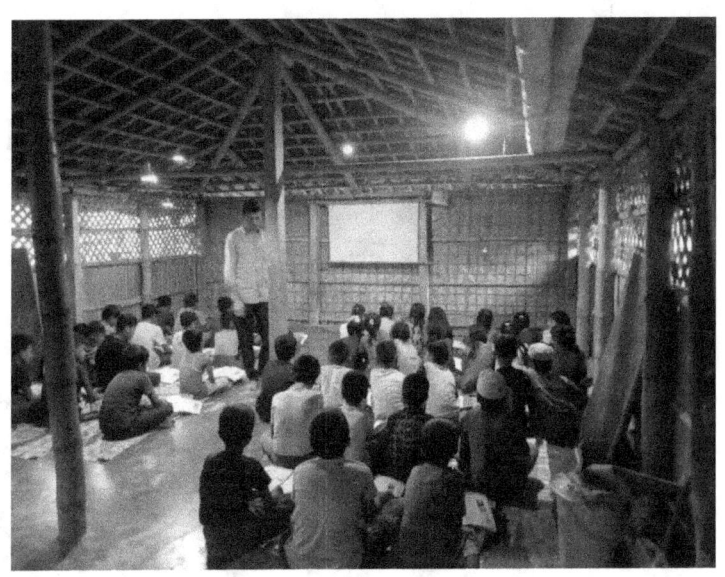

No one chooses to be a refugee. It is imposed by different tyranny governments and people are escaping their own governments." — Ali Saeed

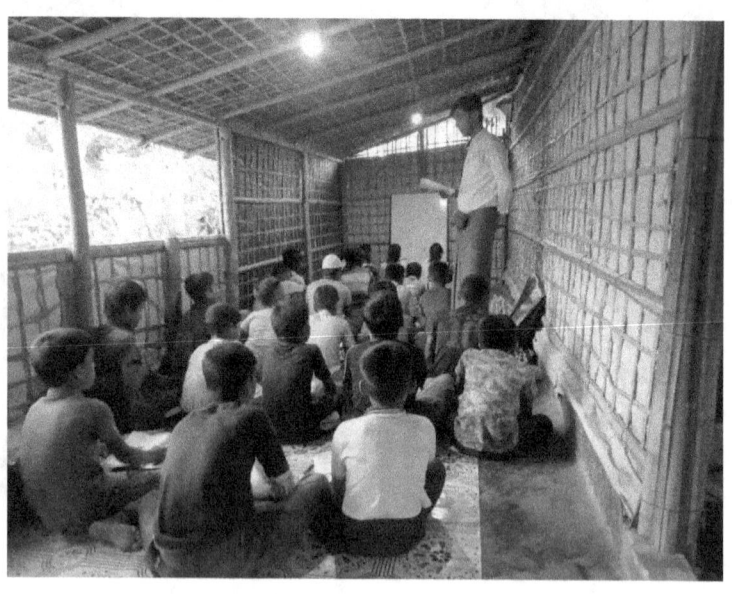

Art is the key that unlocks the doors to possibility

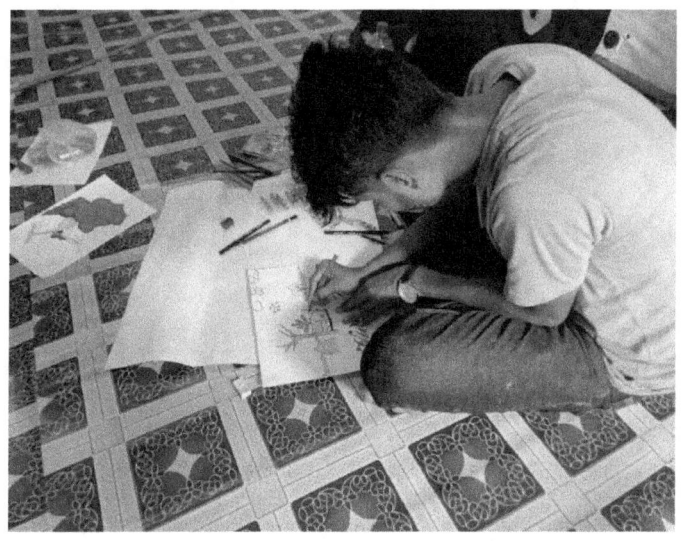

Passion is the North Star that keeps us on course through life's journey

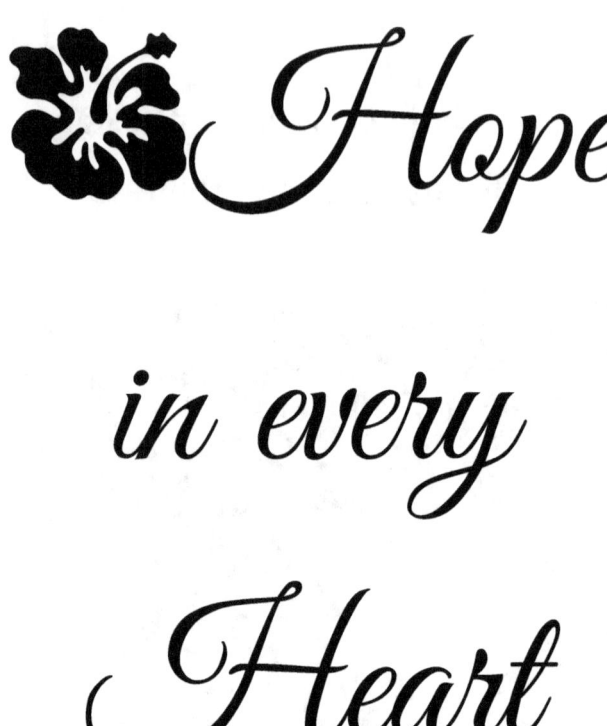

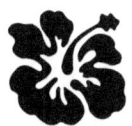

"Internet is a technology that has the ability to get everyone in the world to understand each other."
~Snowden (movie)

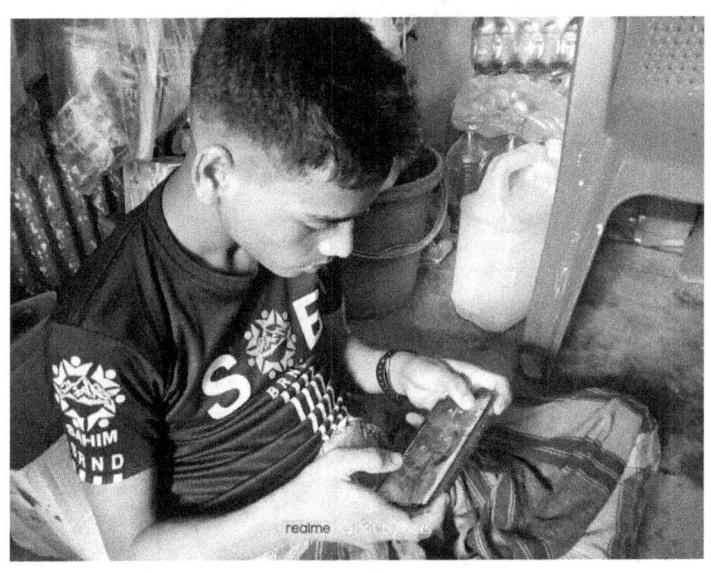

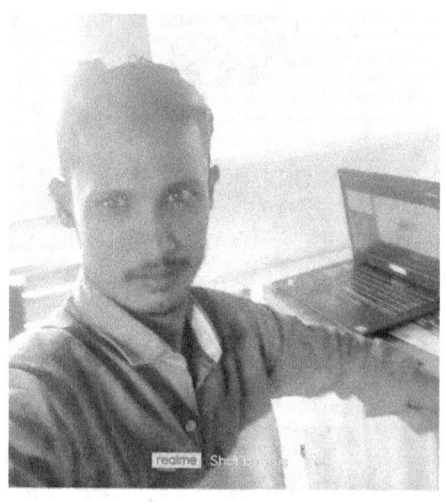

Renewed hope, the beacon that guides us through the darkest storms.

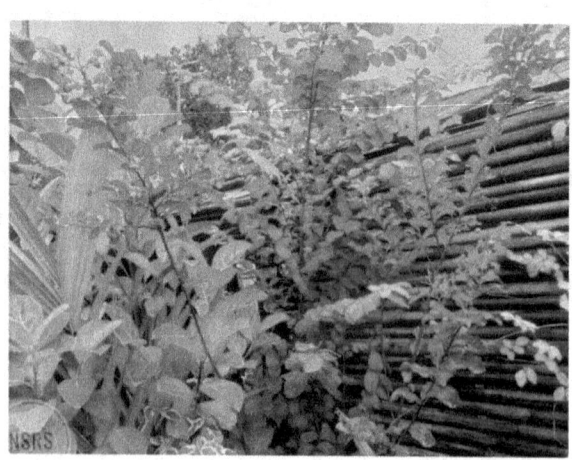

Blooming in Adversity

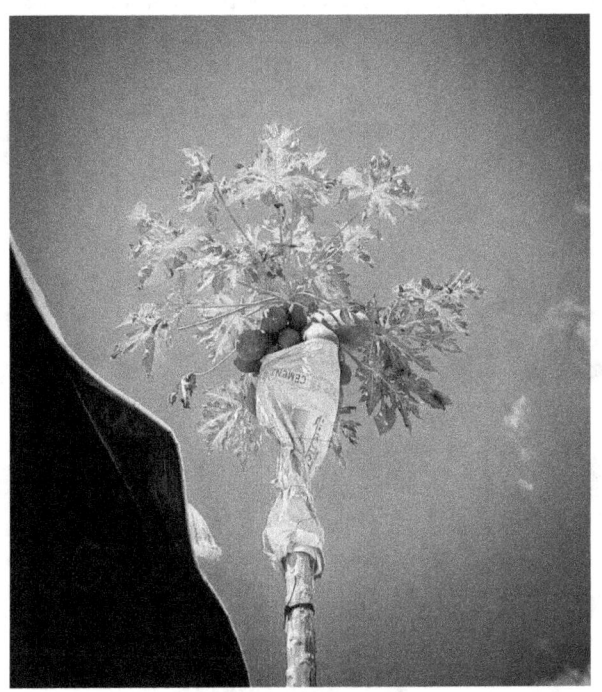

At Cox's Bazar's camp,
where refugees reside.
Like this papaya tree
Hope and Voices rise.

Border of Myanmar and Bangladesh

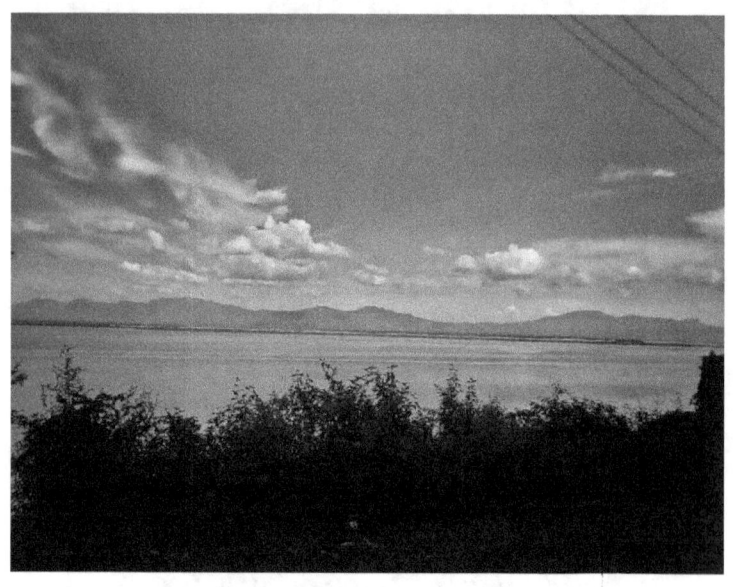

Ah dear home!
I do not know how I will ease my grief!
I'm passing the days just for you; in tears!
I hope that I will be alongside you soon

Hope is the music
that soothes the soul
in times of turmoil

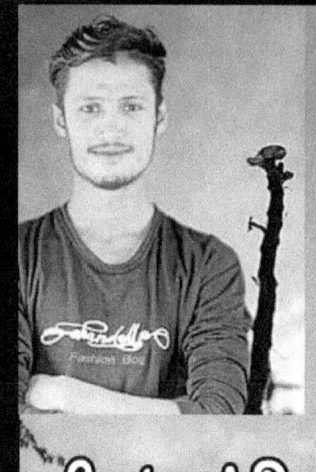

Rohim Ullah is a frontline worker, a photojournalist and videographer.

He has resided at Cox's Bazar, the world's largest refugee camp, since 2017, after escaping ethnic cleansing in Myanmar.

Rohim documents moments of Rohingya refugees to serve as historical records, to raise awareness, and to spark global conversations.

Rohim Ullah

Captured Dreams ~ Rohim Ullah

"Captured Dreams" is more than just photography!

It is a compilation of evocative photos, poems, and quotes, all of which shine a light on the stark reality of Rohingya life.

It's a story of survival, superhuman strength, and suffering of the spirit. It's also a plea for justice, a cry for help, and a call to restore faith in humanity.

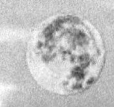

Captured Dreams - An artist's soulful gaze on Rohingya